The t-Shaped Engineer in the Age of AI

The t-Shaped Engineer in the Age of AI

Formation, Vocation, and Christian Education in the Digital Age

MICHAEL J. McGINNIS

RESOURCE *Publications* • Eugene, Oregon

THE t-SHAPED ENGINEER IN THE AGE OF AI
Formation, Vocation, and Christian Education in the Digital Age

Copyright © 2026 Michael J. McGinnis. All rights reserved. Except for brief quotations in critical publications or reviews, no part of this book may be reproduced in any manner without prior written permission from the publisher. Write: Permissions, Wipf and Stock Publishers, 199 W. 8th Ave., Suite 3, Eugene, OR 97401.

Resource Publications
An Imprint of Wipf and Stock Publishers
199 W. 8th Ave., Suite 3
Eugene, OR 97401

www.wipfandstock.com

PAPERBACK ISBN: 979-8-3852-7132-0
HARDCOVER ISBN: 979-8-3852-7133-7
EBOOK ISBN: 979-8-3852-7134-4

01/14/26

Scripture quotations taken from The Holy Bible, New International Version®, NIV®. Copyright © 1973, 1978, 1984, 2011 by Biblica, Inc. Used with permission of Zondervan. All rights reserved worldwide. www.zondervan.com.

To MY BOARD OF DIRECTORS—Roger, Ron, Bryan, Mitch, Paul, and especially Joe, gone too soon. I hope you would be proud of this work. Your wisdom, friendship, and presence have shaped me more than you know.

To TIM KELLER, whose words found me when I was lost. This quote from *The Decline and Renewal of the American Church* became a guiding light:

> There is a robust, respected, and growing community of intellectuals and scholars that hold unashamedly to historic Christian doctrine who are (a) active in every academic field of inquiry, producing scholarship that contributes to and alters the field, (b) a growing presence in universities, and (c) inaugurating an entire alternate intellectual economy of study centers, think tanks, academies, periodicals, and publishing.

I hope this book is a small contribution to that alternate economy. I hope he would be proud. He changed my life. Without him, I might still be lost. I'm so glad to be found.

To MY DAUGHTERS—may you become the kind of engineers described in these pages, with lives full of meaning and purpose. And to my son Joe T., just beginning that journey—I pray you find that meaning and purpose in His Kingdom too.

To MY BEAUTIFUL WIFE ALISON—your warm, winsome faith has been my anchor. You were the first to agree to read this book, and the first to say it was good. Thank you for your enthusiasm, your encouragement, and your belief that I might actually finish a book.
I am so blessed to be your husband.

Contents

Story Index: Personal Narratives and Vignettes | ix
Preface | xi

PART I. DIAGNOSIS: ATTENTION, MEANING AND FORMATION IN CRISIS | 1

Chapter 1: Introduction: Awakening in the Age of AI | 3
Chapter 2: The Digital Age and Cognitive Impacts | 15
Chapter 3: The Crisis of Meaning | 27
Chapter 4: What is Engineering For | 36

PART II. FORMATION IN PRACTICE— BECOMING T-SHAPED IN THE AGE OF AI | 47

Chapter 5: Technical Depth in an Automated World | 51
Chapter 6: A Puzzle Metaphor: How AI Actually Works | 61
Chapter 7: AI in the Classroom—Wisdom in the Classroom for Students and Faculty | 74

PART III. RELATIONAL AND THEOLOGICAL RESPONSE—FORMATION FOR FLOURISHING | 83

Chapter 8: What Has Come Before — Key Voices on AI, Pedagogy, and Formation | 85
Chapter 9: Relational Breadth in a Disconnected Age | 98
Chapter 10: Theological Grounding in a Secular Age | 115
Chapter 11: From 'Have-To' to 'Get-To'—Faculty at the Center | 130

CONTENTS

PART IV. SUMMATION AND VISION— A CALL TO THE BUILDERS | 141

Chapter 12: Formation in the Storm | 143

Chapter 13: The CEO and the Crossroads: A Real World Embodiment | 155

Epilogue: What Are We Building? | 169

Appendix A: A Bit Further Along the Road to How Generative AI Works | 173

Appendix B: AI Initiatives for Formation | 183

Bibliography | 205

Story Index: Personal Narratives and Vignettes

This book is built on stories—moments of insight, failure, grace, and growth. The index below highlights key narratives and where to find them. Use them in your teaching, mentoring, or personal reflection.

Story Title	Chapter	Theme / Use
Convicted in Newberg	Chapter 1	A turning point in the author's AI journey; illustrates the shift from skepticism to conviction.
Two Faculty, One Spark	Chapter 1	Faculty-led transformation; shows how peer leadership can catalyze institutional change.
The Hearth and the Heat	Chapter 1	A retreat metaphor that reframes digital formation; introduces the idea of focal practices.
He Did What?	Chapter 2	A student answers a phone during a presentation; illustrates the erosion of attention.
The Wall Comes Down	Chapter 2	A research trip with a student; highlights grit, perseverance, and technical formation.
Lessons from a Broken Boat	Chapter 2	A concrete canoe team finishes a race with a cracked boat; a vivid metaphor for resilience.
A Misplaced Book and a Found Life	Chapter 3	The author's conversion story; a deeply personal account of finding faith and meaning.

STORY INDEX: PERSONAL NARRATIVES AND VIGNETTES

Story Title	Chapter	Theme / Use
We Belong	Chapter 3	A student's quiet affirmation after a competition win; speaks to identity and belonging.
Wipe Out	Chapter 4	The author's daughter's academic struggles; illustrates the need for relational and spiritual support.
Softball at the Faculty Retreat	Chapter 5	A lighthearted story about practice and growth; connects to the value of repetition in learning.
How AI Works: A Puzzle Analogy	Chapter 6	How my family's puzzle obsession reflects the mechanics of AI
One Slide, One Story	Chapter 7	A moment of technological failure that led to unexpected clarity and connection.
Batch by Batch	Chapter 8	A daughter's science fair project; metaphor for formation and iteration.
My Personal Board of Directors	Chapter 9	Introduces key mentors; models the importance of relational breadth and mentorship.
The World's Greatest Banana Salesman	Chapter 10	A humorous classroom parable; reframes education as a "get-to" rather than a "have-to."
A Dear Friend (Mike Gangone)	Chapter 11	A colleague's influence; introduces the "get-to" mindset and the power of faculty culture.
Something to Say	Chapter 12	A mentor's legacy; underscores the spiritual depth behind leadership and formation.
A Gentle Reminder	Chapter 13	A gentle correction highlights the power of emotional intelligence and presence
Mike Mulligan	Epilogue	A description of the power of story and the impact of a children's book on the author's life and career.

Preface

To introduce this book, I'm going to introduce you—just a bit—to me. My wife and I met after seasons of brokenness and loss. We've built a blended family and worked toward redemption, trying to keep God at the center. This is a story of how we met—and a glimpse of the "whole story."

We met online. Yes, the person who will be pointing out some of the perils of the current digital ecosystem in just a few pages met the love of his life on-line. It was a simpler time back then—nearly 15 years ago.

We traded emails, she's a wonderful writer. I'd seen her picture, she is stunningly beautiful. We'd connected on the phone several times. What a conversationalist. And her faith: warm, approachable, gentle. Full of grace.

Our relationship started slowly. It took time to see the whole story. But we did. And we've gone on to build a life together. We keep God at the middle of our marriage. She's gone back to school and works as a mental health counselor in a high school. We both feel like we are in God's calling, pouring into the next generation, into our family, into each other. We're writing the rest of the story together. I love her so very much.

If I'd let the slow start win the day, if I hadn't had the patience to see more of the story, I would have missed it.

This preface is an invitation: slow down, take in the whole story, and let it form you.

WHAT THE BOOK IS

The t-Shaped Engineer in the Age of AI is a book about formation. It's about what it means to become—not just a better engineer, but a wiser human—in a time when digital tools are reshaping everything.

It's built around a simple but powerful model: the **t-shaped engineer**.

- **Technical Depth**: the foundation of engineering competence.
- **Relational Breadth**: the skills that help us connect, lead, and serve.
- **Christ-Centered Purpose**: the anchor that reminds us who we are and whose we are.

The shape matters. It's a cross. And that's not accidental.

WHAT THE BOOK OFFERS

The book unfolds in four parts:

1. **Diagnosis**: What's happening in the age of AI—and why it matters for formation.
2. **Technical Response**: How we can teach and learn with depth, rigor, and discernment.
3. **Relational & Theological Response**: How we build people, not just pipelines.
4. **Summation & Vision**: A call to action—and a glimpse of what's possible.

Along the way, you'll find:

- A 2x2 matrix for navigating AI and learning posture
- Five strategic initiatives for engineering education
- Over a dozen personal stories
- A structured interview with a Christian CEO wrestling with AI in real time
- A theological-pedagogical framework for formation in the digital age
- Two appendices, a story index, and a pastoral resource for educators

WHY IT MATTERS

This isn't just a book for engineers. This isn't just a book about AI. It's a book about attention, meaning, grit, and grace. It's about what happens when we slow down, look again, and commit to seeing the whole story. It's a book for anyone who cares about formation, vocation, and the future of learning. It's a book for teachers, mentors, leaders, and learners.

PREFACE

It's a book for people who believe that wisdom still matters—and that story is one of the best ways to find it.

Whether you're an engineer, educator, student, or simply someone seeking wisdom in a noisy world—welcome. I hope this book helps you see more of the story. And I hope it helps you as you write your own.

PART I

Diagnosis: Attention, Meaning and Formation in Crisis

CHAPTER 1

Introduction: Awakening in the Age of AI

LATE TO THE PARTY, RIGHT ON TIME: A TIMELINE OF AWAKENING

36 months ago

I barely knew AI existed.

24 months ago

My attitude was essentially:
"AI? Whatever. Probably no big deal."

18 months ago

AI is probably something big.

12 Months ago:

A bigger shift began.
AI might be transformative. Its use could be widespread.
And it's going to impact what it means to be human.

PART I. DIAGNOSIS

CONVICTED IN NEWBERG

Twelve months ago, I attended the 2024 Christian Engineering Conference in Newberg, Oregon—a gathering of people who care deeply about transforming the lives of engineering students. It was the kind of conference I love: small enough to foster real connection, large enough to feel the weight of shared purpose.

I was presenting a paper on leadership transitions in engineering departments, co-written with my Associate Dean. I had also organized and chaired a meeting of leaders from over 20 Christian engineering programs to discuss the future of our work. I was looking forward to all of it—except one thing.

The keynote was on AI.

To be honest, I wasn't that excited. I wasn't even that curious. I was skeptical, maybe even dismissive. AI felt like a buzzword, a distraction from the real work of education and transforming student lives. A little part of me planned to attend the keynote out of obligation, not interest.

Then Jacob Shatzer took the stage.

A theologian from Union University, Jacob didn't talk about algorithms or automation. He talked about what it means to be human. He asked whether we were losing something essential—our telos, our purpose—in the digital age. He warned that technology, if left unexamined, could be co-opted by a gospel that is not our own.

And I was convicted. Deeply.

This was the first moment I realized I needed to respond—not just as an educator, but as a Christian. Not just with curiosity, but with conviction. AI wasn't just a technical issue. It was a formational one. And I had work to do.

9 months ago

"Yes, this is real—and important."
But I'm not that kind of engineer.
I'm a rocks-sand-gravel engineer.
This AI thing? Someone else's problem.

INTRODUCTION: AWAKENING IN THE AGE OF AI

6 months ago

Actually, I'm the Dean of Engineering at *the* Christian Polytechnic University.

And it's starting to feel like professional malpractice not to have an educated opinion—or a suggested approach.

TWO FACULTY, ONE SPARK

Six months ago, we were riding the momentum of a transformative school-wide teaching workshop. To keep that energy alive, we launched a series of monthly lunch-and-learns—spaces for faculty to gather, share ideas, and build a culture of thoughtful, student-centered teaching.

At first, I led them. But the goal was always to hand them off—to let faculty take ownership. That fall, Andrew Davis volunteered to lead a session. He brought along Chad File. What they shared changed everything.

Andrew is a machine learning expert, PhD-trained and deeply technical. Chad had been experimenting with AI tools in his own work. Together, they offered a session that was part demonstration, part invitation. Andrew showed us the math and science behind AI. Chad showed us its power—how it could help us teach, write, and even manage the administrative load of academic life.

It was, once again, convicting.

This wasn't just a curiosity. It wasn't a passing trend. It was a tool with real implications for how we teach, how we lead, and how we form students. That lunch-and-learn didn't just inform me—it moved me. It helped shift my posture from cautious observer to committed participant.

3 months ago

I committed: AI and its impact on engineering education would be one of our Big Three Strategic Priorities for 2025–2026.

2 months ago

I began preparing faculty development workshops.
I committed to using AI—not just talking about it.

PART I. DIAGNOSIS

To understand it well, I had to become an experienced user. To know its strengths. To know its limits.

THE HEARTH AND THE HEAT

Two months ago, I was selected to attend a Christian retreat on discipleship in the digital age. Over 80 people at our university applied—only 20 were chosen. I was honored to be among them.

The retreat was led by Jonathan Lett, my coauthor on the first paper introducing the t-shaped engineer. Jonathan is a theologian—brilliant, thoughtful, sometimes lofty in language. But not here. At this retreat, he was grounded, relatable, vulnerable. A gifted facilitator. He curated an amazing experience.

We explored how the digital world is shaping us—how it forms our habits, our attention, even our desires. One metaphor in particular stayed with me: the hearth.

In pre-modern homes, the hearth was the focal point—the source of warmth, light, and life. But it took effort. You had to gather wood, tend the fire, keep it going. It was a communal task. A focal practice. And that was the point: some things aren't meant to be rushed. They're meant to be done slowly, together, with care.

That image broke something open in me.

We talked about the good things the digital age offers—but also the ways it tempts us to trade depth for speed, presence for performance. In particular, what a precious resource and gift our attention is. We talked about being dedicated children of God in the current moment. After several days of marinating in these ideas, something shifted. The abstract, the journal article, the book—they all began to pour out of me.

This retreat didn't just inform me. It re-formed me.

This month

While prepping for a workshop, I realized I had the bones of a great conference talk.
Then I realized I had something more:

INTRODUCTION: AWAKENING IN THE AGE OF AI

Something important to say.
I wrote an abstract.
Then a paper.
And now, this book.

Today

I'm sitting in a meeting of Deans.
Someone suggests using Office 365 to track changes and "combat AI."
Another Dean, in a side conversation:
"Every email I get, every opportunity—it's all about AI."
Then she adds, almost offhand:
"I'm tired. I'm thinking about retirement more than ever."
And I get it.
But for me—

I'd love to say the time for this book is now.
But truthfully?
This book is late.
I just hope it's not too late.

WHY THIS BOOK, WHY ME

I've spent the last several years thinking deeply about where engineering education is going. I've watched students struggle—not just with equations, but with meaning. I've seen faculty burn out—not just from workload, but from a loss of vocational clarity. And I've come to believe that the future of engineering education isn't just about better tools or smarter machines. It's about better formation.

That's where the *t-shaped engineer* comes in. A model I've been developing for years—one that integrates technical depth, relational breadth, and Christ-centered purpose.

PART I. DIAGNOSIS

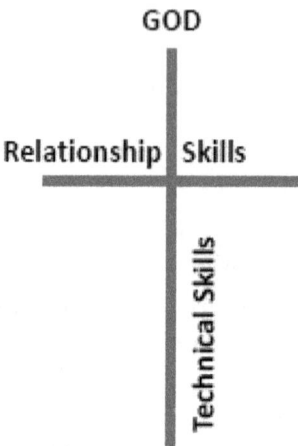

The t-Shaped Engineer

It's not just a framework. It's a way of forming whole people in a fragmented world. And as AI accelerates the pace of change, this model has become more relevant than ever.

We'll explore it in depth soon. But for now, just know: it's the compass I've used to navigate this moment—and the one I'm offering to you.

This book is built on a simple but powerful idea: that engineers need more than technical depth. They need relational breadth. And they need theological grounding. They need to be formed—not just trained. Throughout this book, I'll share stories from my own journey—moments of failure, insight, and unexpected grace—that have shaped how I think about engineering, education, and our calling to transform the entire trajectory of student's lives.

FRAMING THE ROAD AHEAD: A 2X2 MATRIX FOR FORMATION

AI is not just changing how our students learn—it's reshaping how they think, feel, and live. Not long ago, engineering education could begin with a set of assumptions: that students had wrestled with idea generation, persevered through memorization, and developed the grit that comes from iterative problem-solving. We assumed they were preparing for careers that would demand technical expertise layered atop a lifetime of relational practice and a self-directed search for meaning.

INTRODUCTION: AWAKENING IN THE AGE OF AI

But those assumptions are eroding. The convergence of artificial intelligence and the digital life—smartphones, social media, algorithmic feeds—has accelerated a cultural shift marked by shortened attention spans, diminished deep thinking, and a growing epidemic of loneliness, anxiety, and existential drift. Increasingly, students arrive on campus without the tools to sustain intrinsic motivation, build meaningful relationships, or articulate a coherent sense of purpose.

This is not just a pedagogical challenge. It is a spiritual one.

Christian engineering education must respond with clarity and courage. The rise of AI is unprecedented in its speed and scope—by some measures, the fastest-adopted technology in human history.[1] Its impact on professional work, particularly at the entry level, is already reshaping the landscape.[2] Tasks once reserved for junior engineers are now being automated.[3] Efficiency is prized. Fluency with AI tools is assumed.

This presents a dual challenge for Christian educators and students alike. We must navigate two intersecting dimensions:

- The spectrum between **AI-proofing** and **AI-enhancing** educational practices
- The mindset shift from **"have-to"** to **"get-to"** learning

These dimensions form a 2x2 matrix—a simple but powerful tool for reflection and strategy.

The 2x2 matrix is more than a framework. It's a compass, a foundation. It helps us locate where we are—and where we might be headed. It maps two intersecting tensions: whether we resist or embrace AI, and whether we approach learning as a burden or a calling.

Each quadrant tells a story. Each one reflects a posture—toward technology, toward the purpose of education, and ultimately, toward what it means to be human in an age of machines.

Let me walk you through them.

---

1. Microsoft, AI Diffusion Report, 3.
2. Mayer et al. "Generation AI, 598.
3. Advancio, "No Junior Engineers, para. 4.

PART I. DIAGNOSIS

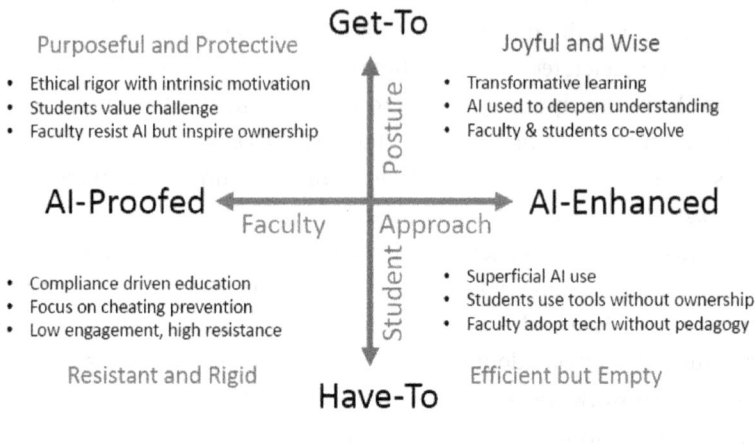

2x2 Matrix

Resistant and Rigid

(AI-Proofing + Have-To)

This is the "no AI allowed" zone. It's often born from fear—of cheating, of change, of losing control. Faculty in this space may ban AI outright, hoping to preserve the integrity of learning. Students, in turn, experience education as a series of hoops to jump through. The result? A culture of compliance, not curiosity.

But fear is a poor foundation for growth. When we lead with prohibition, we risk missing the deeper questions: What are we protecting? And what are we forming in its place?

Efficient but Empty

(AI-Enhancing + Have-To)

This quadrant embraces AI—but only as a shortcut. Students use it to finish assignments faster. Faculty use it to streamline grading. Everyone gets more done. But something is lost.

The soul of learning is hollowed out. Reflection is replaced by automation. Struggle is bypassed. And formation—the slow, sacred work of becoming—is quietly abandoned.

INTRODUCTION: AWAKENING IN THE AGE OF AI

This is the danger of efficiency without purpose. It looks productive. But it leaves students unformed.

Purposeful and Protective

(AI-Proofing + Get-To)

Here, AI is resisted—but not out of fear. Out of discernment. Faculty in this space are asking: What is worth preserving? What parts of the learning journey are too sacred to outsource?

This posture protects the spaces where presence matters. Where attention is cultivated. Where students learn to wrestle with ambiguity and grow through effort.

The risk here is isolation—of becoming so cautious that we miss the opportunities AI might offer. But the strength is clarity. This quadrant reminds us that not everything should be automated. Some things are meant to be done slowly, together, with care.

Joyful and Wise

(AI-Enhancing + Get-To)

This is often the goal. The upper-right quadrant. Here, AI is used not to replace thinking, but to deepen it. Students are invited to explore, reflect, and iterate. Faculty become guides, not gatekeepers. Learning is framed not as a task to complete, but as a gift to receive.

This posture requires intentionality. It's not easy. But it's where growth happens. It's where students begin to see their work not just as performance, but as calling. Not just as output, but as offering.

Before we move on, it's worth noting that each axis of this matrix tends to reflect a different center of gravity. The **vertical axis**—from "have-to" to "get-to"—is primarily about **student mindset**: how learners approach their work, whether with obligation or with ownership. The **horizontal axis**—from "AI-proofing" to "AI-enhancing"—leans more toward **faculty posture**: how educators design learning environments, policies, and expectations around AI.

But these aren't hard boundaries. There's overlap. Faculty shape student mindset through the way they teach, the assignments they give, and the culture they create. And students, in turn, influence how AI is

PART I. DIAGNOSIS

used—whether as a shortcut or a springboard. Formation at its best is not a solo act, it's a journey between student and guide.

Each quadrant represents a different posture toward AI and education. Some practices resist AI's influence; others embrace it. Some reinforce obligation; others cultivate joy and purpose. The goal is not to pick one quadrant—but to move toward the upper-right: a space where AI is used wisely, and learning is experienced as a gift.

These are not merely questions of curriculum design. They are questions of anthropology and theology. AI didn't start this conversation. In fact, AI is simply part of a larger constellation that includes smartphones, algorithms and the pace and always on nature of modern digital life.

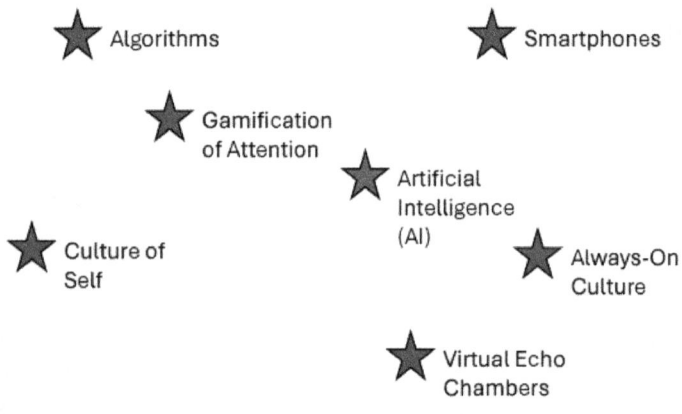

The Malforming Digital Constellation

But it has accelerated it. It has forced us to ask: What does it mean to be human in an age of machines? What are we made for? What is our ultimate purpose? What kind of engineers are we forming? And what kind of people are we becoming?

This book is my attempt to answer those questions—not just as an academic, but as a mentor, a leader, and a person of faith.

WHO IS THIS BOOK FOR?

This book is written first and foremost for Christian educators and administrators—those of us tasked with forming students in a time of rapid technological and cultural change. We need to get out in front of this moment,

INTRODUCTION: AWAKENING IN THE AGE OF AI

not with fear or defensiveness, but with clarity, courage, and hope. It isn't too late—but it's getting close. The choices we make now will shape not only how our students learn, but who they become.

It's also for Christian students. My plea is simple: don't cheat yourself out of formation. AI can be a powerful tool, but it can also be a tempting shortcut. This book is an invitation to wrestle with the deeper questions—about calling, character, and what it means to be human in an age of machines.

And for prospective students and their families: I hope this book helps you ask better questions. Not just "What will I study?" or "Where will I go?" but "Who will I become?" and "Who will walk with me on that journey?" Look for institutions that are engaging this new paradigm with wisdom and intentionality—places where growth of the whole person is not an afterthought, but the foundation.

Finally, in full transparency, I'd be honored if a few non-Christians read this book too. It's not written as an apologetic, but I hope it's gentle, thoughtful, and winsome. If you're curious about how faith intersects with engineering, education, and AI—this is my humble attempt to explore that intersection with honesty and care.

This book is organized into 12 additional chapters, framed by an introduction and epilogue, and supported by two appendices. It begins with a diagnosis of the cultural and cognitive challenges facing students and educators in the digital age—disconnection, anxiety, loneliness, and a crisis of meaning (Chapters 2 and 3). These early chapters are grounded in research and lived experience, offering a clear-eyed look at the formative pressures shaping today's engineering students.

At the heart of the book is a proposed solution: the t-shaped engineer (Chapter 4). This model integrates three essential dimensions—technical depth, relational breadth, and Christ-centered purpose—and is introduced as both a conceptual framework and a practical response to the age of AI. Chapter 6 offers a plain-language explanation of how generative AI works, using a puzzle metaphor to demystify the technology for non-specialists. Chapter 7 builds on this by offering practical wisdom for students and faculty on how to use AI well in the classroom—when it helps, when it hinders, and how to discern the difference. Chapter 8 then surveys key voices in the AI and education landscape, grounding the book's proposals in a broader scholarly and theological conversation.

PART I. DIAGNOSIS

The book then moves from vision to action, offering a roadmap of five strategic initiatives designed to help institutions, faculty, and students navigate this moment with clarity and conviction (explored through reflections on relationship skills—Chapter 9, a theological positioning—Chapter 10, and a commissioning of the faculty at the center of it all—Chapter 11). These initiatives are woven into the t-shaped framework and aligned with the 2x2 matrix that helps readers reflect on their own posture toward AI and learning.

Chapter 12 serves as a culminating reflection—a synthesis of what we've learned, what we still don't know, and a call to action for educators, parents, and leaders. It revisits the book's central frameworks and invites readers to consider how students can flourish even in the midst of cultural and technological storms.

Chapter 13 brings the model out into the marketplace—providing an interview with a Christian CEO. In the interview, Mitch Fortner provides a clear eyed view of the necessity of a t-shaped approach to today's engineering careers.

The book concludes with two appendices. Appendix A provides a more detailed explanation of the science and logic behind how generative AI actually works. Appendix B gathers all of the information about the five formational initiatives that have been proposed across the book into one place, providing additional resources to enable execution of each across a wide variety of institutions. Finally, the bibliography provides a comprehensive list of references cited throughout the book, grounding its insights in a wide range of scholarly, theological, and pedagogical sources.

Throughout, the book is animated by a rich theological vision—one that sees engineering not just as a profession, but as a calling (dispersed throughout but anchored in Chapter 10). It invites readers to consider what it means to be human, to teach and learn with purpose, and to form students who are not only competent, but wise.

CHAPTER 2

The Digital Age and Cognitive Impacts

ATTENTION: THE BATTLE FOR PRESENCE IN A DISTRACTED AGE

He Did What?

Let me tell you a story about student attention.

Earlier in my career, I had a bright student—smart, capable, but not particularly polished. He had a can-do attitude and often a ready, fire, aim outlook. During his senior design mid-year presentation—a high-stakes moment in front of classmates, faculty, and visiting professionals—he stood before the room with his team, delivering their progress report.

Senior Design is a capstone experience. When done well, it embodies all three dimensions of the t-shaped engineer: deep technical challenge, intense team collaboration, and a search for meaning and purpose. It's a space for growth, conflict, and transformation.

In the middle of this charged environment, as his team presented, his phone rang. And he answered it.

Right there, in front of everyone—in a moment that called for professionalism and poise—he took the call.

I was stunned. This was a good student. I liked him. I wanted to help him grow. But this moment felt like a breach of something deeper than etiquette. I failed him on the assignment. Not out of anger, but out of conviction. This was a moment for learning. And it opened the door to a conversation—about attention, presence, and growth.

That moment has stayed with me—not because it was outrageous, but because it was ordinary. In a world saturated with digital stimuli, attention has become a scarce resource. Our students are not just distracted; they are being shaped by distraction. Their cognitive habits, their capacity for sustained focus, even their sense of self—these are all being formed in the crucible of the digital age.

The Shrinking Span

We are living through a cultural compression of attention. Not long ago, we gathered around 2-hour films. Then came 30-minute sitcoms. Then 10-minute YouTube videos. Now, we scroll through 60-second TikToks and 15-second Instagram reels. The medium has changed—and so has the mind.

This isn't just anecdotal. A growing body of research confirms what many educators have sensed: attention spans are shrinking, and the digital environment is a major factor.

A 2024 study in the Eurasian Journal of Applied Linguistics found that frequent exposure to short-form video content significantly reduces students' attention spans and correlates with lower academic performance.[1] The study attributes this to cognitive overload caused by rapid content switching, which impairs students' ability to engage in sustained mental effort.

Another 2024 study published in PNAS Nexus took a more experimental approach. Researchers blocked mobile internet access on students' smartphones for two weeks.[2] The results were striking: students showed significantly improved sustained attention, better mental health, and higher subjective well-being. The cognitive improvement was equivalent to being 10 years younger. In other words, constant digital access is aging our students' minds.

Even passive digital habits—like checking notifications or scrolling during lectures—can erode focus. A study from OxJournal found that Fear of Missing Out (FOMO) was a strong predictor of classroom disengagement.[3] Students weren't just distracted by content—they were distracted by the *possibility* of content.

1. Haliti-Sylaj and Sadiku, "Impact of Short Reels," 60.
2. Castelo et al., "Blocking Mobile Internet," pgafo17.
3. Betteridge et al., "How Does Technology Affect Attention Spans," para. 12.

A qualitative study by Mondal adds further nuance. Students reported that their attention spans in class could drop to just 3–5 minutes due to constant digital interruptions.[4] Many were unaware of the concept of digital detox, and few had strategies for managing their attention.

This is not just about phones. It's about who we are as people, about *whose* we are.

Students are not merely distracted—they are being discipled by distraction. Their neural pathways are being rewired for novelty, not depth; for reaction, not reflection. The digital environment is not neutral—it is shaping the very architecture of attention.

The Myth of Multitasking

Many students believe they can multitask—study while texting, listen to lectures while scrolling. But cognitive science tells a different story. Multitasking is a myth. What we call multitasking is actually task-switching, and it comes at a cost.

Psychologists have found that the human brain is not designed for heavy-duty multitasking. Each time we switch tasks, we incur a "switch cost"—a measurable delay in processing and a drop in performance. In a series of experiments, Rubinstein, Evans, and Meyer demonstrated that even predictable task-switching leads to slower response times and increased error rates.[5] The more complex the task, the greater the cost.

Further research by Lui and Wong identified three distinct cognitive limitations that underlie multitasking costs: (1) response selection, (2) retrieval and maintenance of task information, and (3) task-set reconfiguration.[6] These limitations are not simply a matter of processing speed or intelligence—they reflect deeper constraints in how the brain manages competing demands.

A meta-analysis of 49 studies on media multitasking found that multitasking consistently impairs cognitive outcomes, including memory, comprehension, and problem-solving.[7] While it may enhance short-term engagement or persuasion, it undermines the very skills that deep learning requires.

4. Mondal, "Digital Distraction," 47.
5. Rubinstein, Meyer, and Evans, "Executive Control."
6. Lui and Wong, "Cognitive Costs,"
7. Jeong and Hwang, "Media Multitasking Effects," 601.

PART I. DIAGNOSIS

In engineering education, this is especially dangerous. Deep learning requires sustained attention. It requires wrestling with complexity, holding multiple variables in tension, and persevering through ambiguity. These are not tasks that can be done in the margins of a distracted mind. If we think back to the 2x2 matrix introduced in the introduction, distracted students often use AI either surreptitiously or superficially (depending on the faculty approach in their coursework which may vacillate between attempting to use AI to enhance learning versus prohibiting its use altogether)—as a substitute for focused thinking.

The Addictive Design of Distraction

Why is it so hard to focus? Because our devices are not neutral tools—they are engineered to capture and monetize our attention. Every ping, buzz, and notification is a bid for our brain. And behind those alerts is a carefully designed system that exploits our most ancient neurological wiring.

Psychologist David Greenfield, in his work on internet and smartphone addiction, identifies twelve design features that make digital platforms uniquely addictive.[8] These include variable reward schedules (like slot machines), infinite scrolling, social validation loops, and the illusion of control.

These features activate the brain's reward system, particularly the release of dopamine, reinforcing compulsive checking and scrolling behaviors.

This is not just theory. Neuroscientific studies show that platforms like TikTok, Instagram, and Snapchat stimulate the brain's ventral striatum—a region associated with reward and motivation—especially in adolescents. During early adolescence, dopamine and oxytocin receptors multiply in this region, making young people especially sensitive to social feedback and digital affirmation.[9]

This means that students are not just distracted—they are neurologically conditioned to be. Their brains are being trained to seek novelty, affirmation, and stimulation at the expense of sustained attention, reflection, and presence.

This is not a moral failing. It is a design feature. And it calls for compassion, not condemnation. But it also calls for resistance.

8. Greenfield, "Virtual Addiction."
9. Crone and Konijn, "Media Use and Brain Development."

As educators, we must recognize that we are not just competing with entertainment—we are competing with a system designed to hijack attention. And as Christian educators, we must go further: we must form students who can resist that pull, who can reclaim their attention as a gift to be stewarded, not a commodity to be sold.

The Role of AI

Artificial intelligence adds a new layer to this attention crisis. On one hand, AI tools like ChatGPT or Grammarly can streamline tasks, summarize readings, and generate ideas. But on the other hand, they can deepen the habit of outsourcing cognitive effort.

A 2023 study found that while AI tools improve academic efficiency, they also diminish attention span, critical thinking, and perseverance when overused.[10] Students increasingly favor fast, AI-generated answers over slower, effortful learning processes. This shift reflects a reduction in cognitive perseverance and a preference for heuristic shortcuts—what one study called "a weakening of the mental muscles that support deep learning."

If we are not careful, AI becomes another tool of distraction—another way to avoid the slow, sacred work of thinking. The question is not whether we will use AI. The question is how we will use it—and whether we will remain attentive, discerning, and human in the process.

Christian theology offers a radically different vision of attention. We are not made for fragmentation. We are made for communion. We are made to attend—to God, to others, to the created world. Attention is the posture of love. It is the soil in which wisdom grows.

In Rom 12:2 Paul urges us not to conform to the patterns of this world, but to be transformed by the renewing of our minds. That renewal requires attention. It requires presence. It requires silence, stillness, and the courage to dwell in discomfort.

In the Christian tradition, attention is not just a cognitive skill—it is a spiritual discipline. It is the way we behold beauty, receive truth, and respond to God's call.

John Piper, in his book *Think: The Life of the Mind and the Love of God*, argues that thinking is not opposed to faith—it is essential to it.[11] From 2 Tim 2:7: "Think over what I say, for the Lord will give you understanding."

10. Zhai, Wibowo, and Li, "Effects of Over-Reliance," 4.
11. Piper, *Think*, 45.

Piper insists that careful thinking and divine illumination are not enemies but partners. We are called to engage our minds fully, trusting that God meets us in that effort.

Similarly, a 2025 article in *Christianity Today* laments the atrophy of the Christian mind in an age of distraction.[12] Abby McCloskey writes that "distraction crowds out serious thought and engagement," and warns that a weak and disordered evangelical mind is fertile ground for confusion and chaos. She echoes Mark Noll's famous critique in *The Scandal of the Evangelical Mind*, urging believers to recover the discipline of deep, sustained thought as an act of discipleship.[13]

These voices remind us that attention is not merely about productivity—it is about formation. To attend is to love. To focus is to worship. And to cultivate a mind capable of sustained attention is to prepare the soil for wisdom, discernment, and joy.

In this light, the erosion of attention is not just a pedagogical crisis—it is a spiritual one. It is not just that students can't focus; it's that they are being formed in ways that make it harder to love God with all their mind.

ITERATION AND GRIT

The Wall Comes Down

One of the best undergraduates I ever encountered was Michael Lisk. He was bright, but what really made him stand out was his can-do attitude and a never-quit spirit. He was so good that I brought him on a research trip to a prestigious university to help conduct a series of high-stakes experiments.

The goal was to simulate how concrete walls perform under fire conditions. The lab had been retrofitted with a massive furnace and a complex ventilation system—chilled water lines, roof modifications, the works.

Michael was just a sophomore at the time. Our job was to monitor the walls using three advanced technologies: nuclear magnetic resonance imaging to track water movement in the concrete, digital image correlation to measure displacement and cracking, and thermal imaging to capture heat transfer. Each system was intricate, fiddly, and time-consuming to calibrate. It took hours of tedious, focused work just to get ready for a

---

12. McCloskey, "Atrophy of the Christian Mind."
13. Noll, Scandal of the Evangelical Mind.

single test. Much of the work was iterative—try something, get closer to the answer, try again, and again. Until it works, until it is right.

The first test went smoothly—hot, gritty, and exhausting, but successful. Then the chill water system failed. We were stuck for eight hours, troubleshooting and waiting. Michael never wavered. He stayed focused, patient, and engaged.

Finally, we got the second test running. The furnace roared to life. The wall heated up. And then—it exploded.

Shards of hot concrete rained down on our equipment. The wall, built with only one layer of steel reinforcement (technically code-compliant, but less robust than the typical two layers), buckled and tore itself apart. But because of Michael's grit and attention to detail, we captured the data. That data helped us contribute to the team proposing changes to the design code—changes that could make future structures safer.

I don't believe every student today would have had the patience to get that work done. The conditions were miserable, monotonous, and mentally taxing. But they were necessary. And they revealed something essential—not just about engineering, but about character.

The Disappearance of Struggle

In the past, problem-solving involved wrestling with uncertainty. Students had to try, fail, revise, and try again. They had to sit with ambiguity, tolerate frustration, and develop the resilience that comes from effort.

Now, answers are at their fingertips. AI tools like ChatGPT, Wolfram Alpha, and GitHub Copilot can generate solutions in seconds. And while these tools are powerful, they can also short-circuit the very process that builds understanding.

A 2024 study by Zhai, Wibowo, and Li found that students who relied heavily on AI dialogue systems showed a measurable decline in critical thinking, decision-making, and analytical reasoning.[14] Another study by Ward et al. found that while AI use improved GPA and reduced study time, it also weakened students' ability to engage in deep, independent learning.[15]

This is not just a shift in tools. It's a shift in how students experience learning—and how they understand themselves in the process.

---

14. Zhai, Wibowo, and Li, "Effects of Over-Reliance."
15. Ward et al., "AI Use and Academic Performance," 115.

PART I. DIAGNOSIS

The Value of Grit

Psychologist Angela Duckworth defines grit as "passion and perseverance for long-term goals."[16] It's what keeps a student debugging code at midnight or reworking a failed prototype for the third time. Grit is not just a personality trait—it's a muscle. And like any muscle, it grows through use.

But grit is hard to cultivate in a culture of instant answers. When students are conditioned to expect speed, ease, and efficiency, they begin to see struggle as a sign of failure rather than a path to growth.

This is where Christian formation offers a counter-narrative.

The Christian Vision of Effort and Endurance

In the Christian tradition, struggle is not something to be avoided—it is something through which we are shaped. Sanctification is not instant. It is iterative. It is the slow, often painful process of becoming more like Christ.

James 1:2–4 says, "Consider it pure joy, my brothers and sisters, whenever you face trials of many kinds, because you know that the testing of your faith produces perseverance. Let perseverance finish its work so that you may be mature and complete, not lacking anything." (NIV)

This is not just a spiritual truth—it is a pedagogical one. Learning, like sanctification, requires perseverance. It requires the willingness to stay with a problem, to wrestle with it, to let it shape us.

In this light, the disappearance of struggle in education is not just an academic concern—it is a spiritual one. If we remove all friction from the learning process, we risk forming students who are technically proficient but spiritually fragile.

Lessons from a Broken Boat

Some of the most formative stories I've witnessed as an educator have come from the concrete canoe competition (for more information on how the competition works, you can read the 'We Belong' excerpt in Chapter 3). Maybe that's because it's where I've spent so much time. But maybe it's also because the competition itself—structured around technical challenge, team collaboration, and a shared sense of purpose—lends itself so naturally

---

16. Duckworth, *Grit*, 8.

to the kind of maturation we hope to see in our students. This scenario in particular illustrates the power of grit.

This specific story begins with a team that had tasted victory once, but had come up short the last two years. Their captain, determined to reclaim the top spot, poured everything into this year's effort. The boat was a masterpiece—technically sound, beautifully constructed, and visually unforgettable. It was plaid. Yes, plaid. A bold, hideous, glorious royal blue and orange plaid that you could spot from across the lake.

They had written a strong design report. Delivered a solid presentation. It felt like this might be the year. But then came the second-to-last race.

A rogue wave hit mid-course, and one of our paddlers fell out. That was bad enough—they had to swim the boat in, costing precious time. But worse, the boat cracked. Badly. Nearly in half. One whole side was torn open. It looked un-raceable.

The team huddled. The rules allowed duct tape repairs, but at a steep cost: any taped boat would receive a massive deduction in the boat display category. And they knew they had scored well there. The boat was too striking not to.

The final race was the three-person women's endurance event—a long, grueling slalom through buoys to the finish. The team captain gave the three women their orders: "We have to start the race to get the points. But we don't have to finish. Paddle out, start the race, then ditch the boat and swim back."

The other teams knew our boat was damaged. They also knew we were in the hunt to win the whole thing. So when our team showed up at the start line, there was surprise. Confusion. Admiration.

At the call of "Paddles up," our middle paddler raised hers awkwardly—tucked under one arm, her hands gripping both sides of the boat, physically holding the cracked hull together. The horn sounded. They started.

What no one knew—not the captain, not the coaches, not the other teams—was the look that had passed between the three women before the race. A look that said, "We're not ditching." A look that said, "We will finish what we started." A look that simply said, "We will not quit."

And they didn't. One paddled. One steered. One held the boat together. Slowly, steadily, they made their way through the course. My recollection is that they finished fifth out of eleven—not bad for a broken boat.

But what I remember most is the sound. The cheers. The moment when the other teams realized what was happening. The loudest applause of the day wasn't for the fastest boat. It was for the broken one. The one that shouldn't have finished. The one that did. Because sometimes, the most impressive thing isn't how fast you go. It's that you don't give up.

The Role of AI: Tool or Temptation?

AI is not the enemy. It is a tool. But like any tool, it must be used wisely. When AI is used to supplement thinking, it can be a powerful ally. But when it is used to replace thinking, it becomes a shortcut that undermines healthy growth and maturation.

The question is not whether students will use AI. The question is whether they will use it in ways that build grit—or bypass it.

As educators, we must help students see that struggle is not a sign of weakness. It is a sign of growth. And we must design learning environments that reward perseverance, not just performance.

The upper-right quadrant of our 2x2 matrix—Joyful and Wise—represents more than a pedagogical sweet spot. It's a spiritual posture: one that sees learning not as a burden, but as a calling. And this also aligns well with the basic theories of cognitive development.

BLOOM'S TAXONOMY IN THE AGE OF AI: A FRAGILE LADDER

In 1956, Benjamin Bloom and his colleagues introduced a framework that would shape education for decades: Bloom's Taxonomy.[17] It offered a hierarchical model of cognitive skills, from basic recall to complex creation:

1. **Remembering** – recalling facts and basic concepts
2. **Understanding** – explaining ideas or concepts
3. **Applying** – using information in new situations
4. **Analyzing** – drawing connections among ideas
5. **Evaluating** – justifying a decision or course of action
6. **Creating** – producing new or original work

---

17. Bloom, *Taxonomy of Educational Objectives.*

This taxonomy has become a staple in curriculum design, assessment, and pedagogy. But it's not without its critics.

Some cognitive scientists and educators argue that thinking doesn't unfold in neat layers. They suggest that all levels of cognition are interwoven—that even basic recall can involve analysis, and that creation often draws on memory and understanding in complex, nonlinear ways. Others propose alternative models, such as Anderson and Krathwohl's revised taxonomy,[18] Fink's Taxonomy of Significant Learning,[19] or Marzano's Dimensions of Learning, which emphasize integration, affective domains, or metacognition.[20]

These critiques are valid. No model perfectly captures the full complexity of human thought. But models don't need to be perfect to be useful. Like a map, a good model simplifies reality in order to help us navigate it. Bloom's Taxonomy remains a helpful tool—not because it captures every nuance of cognition, but because it gives us a shared language for thinking about learning goals and cognitive development.

And in the age of AI, it gives us something else: a warning.

AI tools like ChatGPT, Wolfram Alpha, and Grammarly now perform the lower levels of Bloom's Taxonomy with astonishing speed and fluency. They can recall facts, summarize texts, solve equations, and even apply formulas to novel problems. What once required hours of study and repetition can now be done in seconds with a well-crafted prompt.

At first glance, this seems like a gift. Why not outsource the tedious parts of learning and focus on the higher-order skills? But here's the problem: the lower rungs are not optional. *They are foundational.* They are the scaffolding that supports everything above.

When students skip the struggle of remembering, understanding, and applying, they lose more than time—they lose the opportunity for healthy growth and change. They miss the slow, effortful process by which knowledge becomes intuition, by which facts become frameworks, and by which ideas become tools for wisdom.

Cognitive science confirms this.[21] The process of encoding information through repetition, retrieval, and application literally rewires the brain. It builds the neural architecture that makes analysis, evaluation, and

18. Anderson and Krathwohl, *Taxonomy for Learning*.
19. Fink, *Creating Significant Learning Experiences*.
20. Marzano, *Dimensions of Learning*.
21. Larsen, "Planning Education for Long-Term Retention," 451.

creation possible. Without that foundation, students may be able to critique—but not comprehend. Remix—but not originate.

This is not just a pedagogical concern. It is a spiritual one.

In the Christian tradition, learning is not merely the acquisition of information—it is the formation of the person. The mind is not a machine to be optimized, but a faculty to be renewed (Rom 12:2). When we bypass the struggle of learning, we risk bypassing the very process by which character, wisdom, and humility are formed.

If we are not careful, AI will become a shortcut that short-circuits maturation and the development of wisdom. It will offer the illusion of mastery without the substance. It will produce students who can generate answers but not ask good questions—who can perform but not persevere.

As educators, we must resist the temptation to treat AI as a replacement for thinking. Instead, we must teach students to use it as a tool for deeper engagement. We must help them see that the lower rungs of Bloom's ladder are not beneath them—they are beneath everything.

And as Christian educators, we must go further. We must remind our students that the goal of learning is not just to know more, but to become more. To become people of wisdom, gratitude, and love. To become engineers who can not only solve problems, but also discern which problems are worth solving.

In the age of AI, Bloom's Taxonomy is not obsolete. Our focus will need to be in ensuring that students' posture leans toward an attitude of privilege in getting to explore information in ways that lead to mastery and formation, that finds the upper right quadrant of our 2x2 framework—and educators will have to ensure that they play their role in this development as well.

The erosion of attention and grit in the digital age is not just a cognitive concern—it is a spiritual one. When students lose the ability to focus and persevere, they also lose the capacity to reflect, to wrestle, and to grow. But beneath this erosion lies something deeper: a quiet ache for purpose. As we turn to the next chapter, we'll explore what happens when that ache is left unanswered—when students no longer know what they're for. Because attention is not just about presence. It's about meaning. And meaning, in the age of AI, is the next frontier of formation.

CHAPTER 3

The Crisis of Meaning

A MISPLACED BOOK AND A FOUND LIFE

I'm going to tell you about my own crisis of meaning. How I became a Christian. It's painful and raw. I'm still not sure it belongs in a book like this. But I'm writing it here because maybe it will help someone else wrestle with the questions that matter most.

My marriage was ending. I don't think I could have said it out loud at the time, but I knew. I had a good life on paper—advanced degrees, a wife, two kids, a job I loved, respect at work. But something was broken. My former wife said to me during that time, "Your work gets the best of you, and I get what's left." That line stuck. It probably has some truth to it. Maybe even some bearing on this book.

I'd grown up in a Christmas-and-Easter kind of home. Some vague sense of God, but no depth. I would've called myself agnostic—felt like something was out there, but I didn't know what. I was so lonely. We'd been sleeping in separate bedrooms for months that turned into years. I was trying to be the best parent I could, putting on a face for the kids. But inside, I broke.

One night, on a business trip, I wandered into a Barnes & Noble to kill time. I ended up in the sci-fi section—my usual escape. But there,

PART I. DIAGNOSIS

mis-shelved at eye level, was a book that didn't belong: *The Reason for God* by Tim Keller.[1] I picked it up. I started reading. And I couldn't stop.

Keller's idea of "doubting your doubts" hit me hard. He didn't argue like he was trying to win. He reasoned like someone who cared. That book led me to *Mere Christianity* by C.S. Lewis.[2] That man could write. And he could logic. Two men, decades apart, writing about meaning and purpose and divine truth with grace and humility. I didn't feel belittled. I felt invited.

From the outside, the Christian community had always looked intimidating. I wasn't sure I could ever be an insider. But for the first time, I saw the evidence. I saw how Christianity made sense of the world as it actually is. I saw that the whole "science versus faith" thing was a false argument—like comparing a pit bull to Beethoven's Fifth Symphony. They're not the same thing. They're not even trying to be.

Long story short: I found God in those dark days. Or maybe He found me. I hate to think He had to take my marriage away to get my attention—and I know it doesn't work like that, so please don't call the theology police—but I'm grateful. Grateful to be His. Grateful to have a purpose. To know what my life is for.

I share this story not because every student I teach is walking the same path—but because many are asking the same questions. What is my life for? What do I do when the scaffolding collapses? Where do I find meaning that holds? They may not say it out loud. They may not even know how to name it. But beneath the distraction, the anxiety, the performance, there is often a quiet ache for purpose. And if we, as educators and mentors, don't speak to that ache—if we don't offer something deeper than technique—we risk forming students who are technically excellent but spiritually adrift.

If the last chapter explored the erosion of attention, this chapter asks what happens when the erosion goes deeper—when it reaches the foundations of identity, purpose, and belief. What happens when students no longer know what they're for?

For Christians, meaning is not something we invent. It is something we receive. It is rooted in our *telos*—our God-given purpose. The Greek word *telos* means "end," "goal," or "completion"—it represents the ultimate purpose for which we as humans were created. It's not just where we're going; it's what we're for. I'll come back to this concept many times throughout this book.

1. Keller, *The Reason for God*.
2. Lewis, *Mere Christianity*.

But in the modern world, telos has been replaced by technique. Formation has been replaced by performance. Students are told to "make their own meaning," to "follow their truth," to "be their authentic self." But what happens when they don't know where to start? What happens when the structure collapses?

Philosopher Charles Taylor describes this as the condition of the "buffered self"—a self sealed off from transcendence, tasked with constructing its own identity in a world that no longer offers it as given.[3] In this secular age, belief in God is no longer the default. It is one option among many. And for many students, it's not even on the menu.

The result is a generation that is spiritually hungry but theologically malnourished. They are not hostile to faith. They are simply unacquainted with it. They are searching for meaning in all the places our culture tells them to look: achievement, activism, aesthetics, self-optimization. But these pursuits, while often sincere, are fragile. They offer fragments of purpose, but not a telos.

Sociologist Tara Isabella Burton calls this phenomenon "remixed spirituality." In her book *Strange Rites*, she describes how young adults are cobbling together belief systems from wellness culture, social media, political identity, and personal experience. These new spiritualities are deeply felt—but they lack coherence.[4] They are curated, not revealed. They are expressive, but not formative.

And into this fragmented landscape steps artificial intelligence—offering answers without anchoring, speed without substance, and personalization without purpose. AI can simulate insight, but it cannot offer wisdom. It can generate content, but it cannot generate calling. It mirrors our confusion and amplifies it.

This is why Christian education must do more than deliver content. It must offer students a vision of what their lives are for. It must speak to the ache beneath the performance. It must name the hunger for meaning—not as a psychological curiosity, but as a spiritual reality.

Viktor Frankl, the Holocaust survivor and psychiatrist, wrote that "those who have a 'why' to live can bear almost any 'how.'"[5] His insight is as true in the classroom as it is in the concentration camp. Students who know their telos—who have a sense of calling—are more resilient, more

---

3. Taylor, *A Secular Age*.
4. Burton,.*Strange Rites*.
5. Frankl, *Man's Search for Meaning*.

joyful, and more free. They are not immune to suffering, but they are not undone by it.

Christian education, at its best, helps students discover that "why." It invites them into a story that is bigger than themselves—a story that begins with a Creator, centers on love, and ends in redemption. It teaches them that they are not accidents. They are image-bearers. They are not just thinkers or doers. They are worshipers. And their work—yes, even their engineering—can be an act of love.

THE EPIDEMIC OF DISCONNECTION

We Belong

Early in my academic career, I was heavily involved as a mentor and faculty advisor for our ASCE Concrete Canoe Team. In just our second year of competition, everything broke just right for us (one might argue over the word *"us,"* as this is a student competition—was I really enough a part of the team to include myself in that "us"?).

Backing up, one must understand both the competition and our place in it. The event combines four components into an engineering challenge centered around building a canoe made of concrete (and yes, it floats!):

- Constructing and displaying the final product
- Writing a design report that outlines project management and engineering decisions
- Delivering an oral presentation to highlight communication and storytelling skills
- Competing in a series of races that test athleticism, training, perseverance, and teamwork

In our region are two of the largest civil engineering programs in the country—consistently ranked in the Top 50 by *U.S. News & World Report*. We had just joined the competition the year before, not yet ABET-accredited (engineering programs can't be accredited until they graduate a student, submit a self-assessment, host a site visit, and go through a lengthy review process that takes about 18 months). Our students took it on faith that we'd eventually achieve that status and be able to back-accredit their degrees.

Many of our students were cast-offs and "re-treads"—those who had false starts or faced setbacks at other programs, ending up with us as a last resort or one more try. Our program was initially led by a National Engineering Teacher of the Year (according to ASEE), a retired West Point officer and a true leader of teams and individuals (I'll describe him further in another of these vignettes in Chapter 9). Our program was built differently—emphasizing togetherness, grit, and many of the "softer" skills highlighted elsewhere in this book.

This was the first place I truly exercised and understood the power of relational skills—one of the three pillars of the t-shaped engineering model. Our team was gritty and close-knit, and on the technical side, just good enough (I still remember that the structural analysis we performed—embarrassingly, under my guidance—identified the wrong failure mode that year, a rookie mistake).

And yet, we won.

Everything broke just right, and this band of kids (yes, some in their mid-20s—still kids to me) triumphed, besting teams with football programs that play in 100,000-seat stadiums, while our university might as well have been called "Southwestern State University—City Name."

When they announced the overall winner, our students were ecstatic. They kind of went bonkers—cheering and carrying on. I was standing in front of two of them when the announcement was made, and I'll never forget what one said to the other, almost under his breath. I'm sure he didn't know I was listening.

He said two simple words, quietly, firmly, with conviction and a little bit of wonder:

"We belong."

Small school. Big dreams. Validated right there at the end of a long day in the hot sun.

THE EMOTIONAL TOLL: ANXIETY, DEPRESSION, AND DESPAIR

If the crisis of meaning is the erosion of purpose, then the epidemic of disconnection is the erosion of presence. Students today are not only unsure of what they're for—they're increasingly unsure of how to be with others.

PART I. DIAGNOSIS

More than two decades ago, Robert Putnam's *Bowling Alone* warned of a slow but steady collapse of American communal life.[6] He documented the decline of civic organizations, neighborhood gatherings, and even casual social rituals like bowling leagues. His conclusion was stark: Americans were becoming less connected, less trusting, and more alone.

That trend has only accelerated. Recent studies confirm that friendship is declining—especially among men.[7] The U.S. Surgeon General's 2023 advisory declared loneliness and isolation to be a public health crisis, with effects on mortality comparable to smoking or obesity.[8] In Europe, the data tells a similar story: antidepressant use has more than doubled in the past 20 years, and surveys show rising levels of social disconnectedness across the continent.[9]

Among young people, the picture is even more troubling. The CDC's Youth Risk Behavior Survey reports that nearly one in three teenage girls in the U.S. has seriously considered suicide.[10] Rates of persistent sadness and hopelessness are rising across all racial and ethnic groups. These are not just statistics. They are signals—flares in the night sky—telling us that something is deeply wrong.

And yet, in the midst of this disconnection, students are more digitally connected than ever. They sit at tables together, but their eyes are on their phones. They scroll through curated feeds of other people's lives while struggling to make sense of their own. They are surrounded by images of connection, but starved for the real thing.

And now, AI is accelerating the drift. It's not just that students are distracted by their phones—it's that they're beginning to outsource the very work of relationship. AI writes their texts, crafts their dating profiles, generates their apologies. It simulates empathy without requiring it. It offers the illusion of connection without the cost of presence. And the more we rely on it to mediate our relationships, the more we lose the ability to actually relate. We are training a generation to communicate without listening, to express without understanding, to connect without caring.

This is not just a social problem. It is a existential one. Because relationships are not optional to human flourishing—they are essential. We

6. Putnam, *Bowling Alone*.
7. Cox, "The State of American Friendship."
8. U.S. Department of Health and Human Services, *Our Epidemic of Loneliness*.
9. European Commission, *Comprehensive Approach to Mental Health*.
10. CDC, "Youth Risk Behavior Survey."

are made for communion. We are made in the image of a relational God: Father, Son, and Spirit. To be human is to be with.

The Harvard Study of Adult Development, one of the longest-running longitudinal studies in history, has reached a simple but profound conclusion: good relationships are the strongest predictor of health, happiness, and longevity.[11] Not wealth. Not success. Not even education. Relationships.

This is not just psychology. It is theology. Jesus said the greatest commandment is to love God with all your heart, soul, mind, and strength—and the second is like it: love your neighbor as yourself. Love people. That's not a suggestion. It's a calling.

And yet, in our engineering classrooms and labs, we often treat relationships as secondary—nice if they happen, but not essential to the work. We focus on technical mastery and individual performance. But if we are forming engineers who cannot collaborate, cannot empathize, cannot lead with humility and care, then we are failing to form whole people.

This is why the "relational breadth" of the t-shaped engineer is not just a soft skill. It is a spiritual imperative. It is the outworking of the second great commandment. It is the recognition that engineering is not just about solving problems—it is about serving people.

In a world that tells students to love things, use people, and worship themselves, we are called to teach them to love people, use things wisely, and worship God.[12] That is the path to connection. That is the path to development of what God calls us to be. That is the path to life.

THE SOCIAL SKILLS GAP: EMOTIONAL INTELLIGENCE IN DECLINE

There's a quiet shift happening in the classroom—and even more so in the workplace. Students are arriving with less confidence in face-to-face interaction, less comfort with ambiguity in conversation, and less ability to read the room. They're bright, capable, and technically proficient. But many struggle to make eye contact, to navigate conflict, or to collaborate in a team without friction.

I've never had a business leader come back to me and say, "I wish your graduates knew more thermodynamics." But I've heard this more than

---

11. Harvard, "What Makes a Good Life?"
12. Brooks, "Subvert the Culture with Love," para. 5.

PART I. DIAGNOSIS

once: "I can't put them in front of clients." Or, "They don't know how to work on a team." These aren't technical deficiencies. They're relational ones. And they're getting worse.

Students today have grown up in a world where much of their communication is mediated through screens. They text instead of talk. They scroll instead of sit. They curate their digital presence but struggle to be present in real life. Even when they're sitting at the same table, they're often interacting more with their phones than with each other.

This isn't just a generational quirk. It's a formational deficit. Because emotional intelligence—EQ—isn't just a personality trait. It's a skill set. And like any skill, it atrophies when it's not practiced.

EQ includes self-awareness, empathy, emotional regulation, and social skill. It's what allows someone to navigate a difficult conversation, to read a client's unspoken concerns, to lead a team through conflict. And it's increasingly what employers are looking for. In fact, a growing body of research suggests that EQ is a stronger predictor of long-term success than IQ—especially in fields like engineering, where collaboration, communication, and leadership are essential.[13]

But here's the problem: AI doesn't help students grow in EQ. If anything, it makes it easier to avoid the discomfort that builds it. Why wrestle with how to phrase a difficult email when ChatGPT can write it for you? Why learn to read body language when most of your meetings are on Zoom? Why practice empathy when your digital assistant never needs it?

AI is not the enemy. But it is a temptation—to outsource not just thinking, but feeling. To avoid the slow, awkward, beautiful work of becoming human.

And yet, that's exactly the work we're called to. Jesus didn't just teach truth. He embodied love. He didn't just solve problems. He saw people. He wept with them. He ate with them. He touched the untouchable. He listened.

When He was asked to name the greatest commandment, He didn't just say "Love God." He said, "Love your neighbor as yourself." That's not a soft skill. That's a sacred calling.

Engineering, at its best, is an act of love. It's about designing systems, structures, and solutions that serve people. That protect them. That empower them. That help them flourish. And if we're going to form engineers

---

13. Brooks, *Emotional Intelligence in the Workplace*, para. 4; Wilcox, *Emotional Intelligence Is No Soft Skill*, para. 6; Coetzer, *Emotional vs. Cognitive Intelligence*, 12.

who can do that well, we have to teach them more than equations. We have to teach them how to love.

That starts with presence. With empathy. With emotional intelligence. With the courage to look someone in the eye and say, "I see you. I hear you. I'm here to help."

We've covered digital distraction, anxiety, depression, and disconnection. We've explored shrinking attention spans, fragile motivation, and a growing crisis of meaning. This is the world as it is—the landscape our students inhabit, and the context in which formation must occur. But the story doesn't end here. Chapter 4 offers a framework for how to thrive within this world. It fully unpacks the t-shaped engineer model—a vision for technical depth, relational breadth, and theological grounding. It's not just a response. It's a way forward.

CHAPTER 4

What is Engineering For

WIPE OUT

Let's start right here.
My daughter didn't make it at Big State U.
11th in her high school class of over 400. 35 on the ACT. A concrete canoe captain for their team, which won the Texas regional for the first time in ages.
She didn't make it.
This book—hopefully—highlights some of the reasons why.
It was my birthday weekend. We were heading out of town for what I hoped would be a lovely, romantic getaway with my wife. She likes to use car time as get-things-done time. Something had been nagging at both of us. We kept asking our daughter for her grades, and then for the bill for the upcoming semester.
"I'm having trouble with my account."
"I can't download it."
"Computer issues."
She had been through the COVID time—cooped up in her dorm room, not able to physically go to class. Was there real connection?
We called the bursar to get the account number so we could pay. Took a while to get through—call this office, call that office. Finally, about halfway to our destination on country roads, we got a nice person on the line.

"We don't have records of her for next semester," they said. "You'll have to ask your student."

My heart dropped. I work in this business. I knew what that meant. I didn't want to know, but I did.

We called our daughter. Pressed her. She broke.

"Dad, I didn't know what to do. I panicked."

We turned the car around. From one city, from one experience, toward another. I remember it clearly. It was a Thursday. We headed toward her college town—only now, it wasn't. We picked her up. Grabbed her things. It was late. We were oh so worried.

What was happening?

On the long, quiet car ride home, we got more of the story. A story of anxiety. Of depression. Of not being able to get out of bed. Of lack of connection. Of a university where she couldn't even get a meeting with a professor about things that mattered.

Much of this wasn't the university's fault—she had a lot of growing up to do. But still.

During that car ride, we discussed enrolling at another university—my university. A place and a pocket where t-shaped engineers were being formed. Where we treated our kids as people, not numbers.

She decided to give it a try.

We hand-walked her application around campus the next day—the last Friday any student could be added to the rolls for the semester. Literally, the last day. She got registered at 4:52 PM.

I turned my best work friend loose on her (he's for another of these stories, and he's amazing). "Watch out for her. Encourage her. Care for her."

And he did. And we did.

She found connection at the new place. She found a team that brought her in. As with many of the stories in this book, that team was concrete canoe. To the best of my knowledge, she's the only student in our state's history to go to Nationals three straight years, finishing Top 10 in each of them.

And yet, she washed out at Big State U.

They may have done the technical parts of engineering education well. But she needed more. Much more.

Relationships. Meaning. Purpose. Care.

She needed them.

This book is one of the ways I'm trying to get that right for the next generation. It will be harder still for them. AI will make it harder on these fronts.

TEACHING ENGINEERING: WHERE WE'VE BEEN

The story you just read is not an isolated case. It reflects a broader pattern in engineering education—one where technical rigor is emphasized, but relational and formational dimensions are often underdeveloped or absent altogether. To understand how we got here, it's worth briefly surveying a few representative models that have shaped engineering pedagogy in recent decades.

Wankat and Oreovicz offered one of the earliest comprehensive guides to engineering education.[1] Their work cataloged a wide range of best practices, from structured lectures to active learning techniques. These methods were largely focused on the **technical transmission of knowledge**, though they did acknowledge the importance of student engagement and classroom rapport.

Technical	Relational
Guide through lesson objectives	Provide prompt and positive feedback
Provide structure and organization	Have positive expectations of students
Use images and visual learning	Challenge, but set them up for success
Ensure the student is active	Make the class cooperative
Require problem solving and repetition	Encourage them to teach one another
Use a variety of teaching styles	Care about what they are doing
Ask thought provoking questions	
Be enthusiastic	

Wankat and Oreovitz Engineering Teaching Techniques

Joseph Lowman introduced a two-dimensional model of teaching effectiveness that has had lasting influence.[2] His framework emphasized:

- **Intellectual Excitement**: clarity of presentation and emotional stimulation

1. Wankat and Oreovicz, *Teaching Engineering*.
2. Lowman, *Mastering the Techniques of Teaching*.

- **Interpersonal Rapport**: the instructor's ability to connect with students and foster motivation

		INTERPERSONAL RAPPORT		
		Low	Moderate	High
INTELLECTUAL EXCITEMENT	High	6. Intellectual Authority	8. Exemplary Lecturer	9. Complete Exemplar
	Moderate	3. Adequate	5. Competent	7. Exemplary Facilitator
	Low	1. Inadequate	2. Marginal	4. Socratic

Lowman's 2-Dimensional Teaching Model (from Estes et al. 2005)

This model helped shift the conversation toward **relational dynamics** in the classroom, recognizing that teaching is not just about content delivery but also about emotional and motivational presence.

The **ExCEEd Teaching Model**, with one of the earliest publications by Estes, Welch, and Ressler, built directly on Lowman's work, while integrating many of the techniques championed by Wankat and Orievicz.[3] It became an important part of the civil engineering education landscape, training hundreds of professors and emphasizing:

- Structured organization
- Engaging presentation
- Enthusiasm
- Positive rapport
- Frequent assessment
- Appropriate use of technology

While ExCEEd brought much-needed attention to **student engagement and feedback**, it still largely operated within a framework that prioritized **performance and delivery** over **purpose and identity**.

In reviewing these models, a pattern emerges: most focus on the **technical** aspects of teaching. Some go beyond this and acknowledge the

---

3. Estes, Welch, and Ressler, "The ExCEEd Teaching Model."

importance of **relationships**. Few, if any, address the deeper questions of **meaning and purpose, of our ultimate telos**. They help us teach well—but they don't help us ask why we teach, or what kind of people we are forming.

This is the gap the **t-shaped engineer model** seeks to fill. It affirms the value of technical depth and relational breadth—but insists that these must be grounded in a theological vision of vocation, identity, and human flourishing.

A Personal Note

One of the prime movers behind the ExCEEd model is Dr. Ron Welch. He also happens to be the man who hired me into the academic side of the engineering profession. One of the best teachers and leaders I've ever encountered. By far.

As I was developing the t-shaped engineer concept, I called Ron. I asked him about meaning and purpose within the ExCEEd model. He told me it was there. I gently said I thought it wasn't.

He laughed and said, "Sure it is."

It was a warm conversation.

We talked again a few weeks later. "Mike—you're right. It isn't really there. It's up to you. Do something about it. Make it happen. You can do it."

That's Ron. (He'll pop up again in this book, don't worry.) Warm, relational, decisive.

THE t-SHAPED ENGINEER: A MODEL FOR FORMATION

If the dominant models of engineering education have helped us teach more clearly and connect more effectively, they have still left a critical question largely unanswered: What is engineering for?

In response to this gap, we propose a model that integrates three essential dimensions of engineering formation: technical depth, relational breadth, and theological grounding. This model is shaped like a lowercase "t"—a deliberate visual and theological choice.

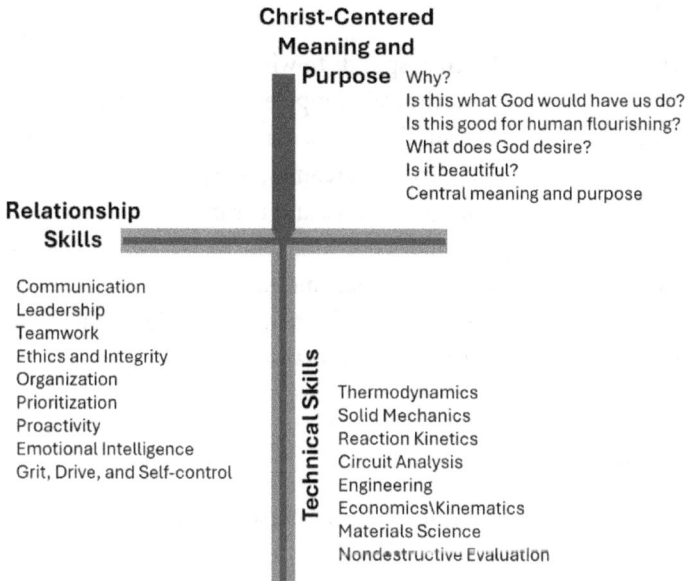

The t-Shaped Engineer

Why the Lowercase "t"?

The lowercase "t" is not just a typographic flourish. It is a symbol of integration. The vertical bar represents technical mastery—the kind of deep disciplinary knowledge that every engineer must possess. The horizontal bar represents relational fluency—the ability to collaborate, communicate, and lead with empathy and integrity. And the upward extension, forming the shape of a cross, represents theological grounding—a faith-informed purpose rooted in the love of God and neighbor.

This model is not merely a metaphor. It is a framework for rethinking curriculum, pedagogy, and institutional culture. It affirms that engineering is a holy calling—a way of bearing God's image by stewarding creation, serving communities, and seeking justice through design.

PART I. DIAGNOSIS

Technical Depth

The vertical bar of the "t" corresponds to what most engineering programs already do well: develop technical competence. This includes mastery of core concepts such as thermodynamics, statics, circuits, and materials. It aligns with several ABET student outcomes, including the ability to apply engineering principles, design systems, and use modern tools.

But technical depth alone is not sufficient. In fact, when isolated from broader human concerns, it can become dangerous. Engineers who are technically brilliant but ethically uninformed may design systems that are efficient but unjust, powerful but dehumanizing.

Relational Breadth

The horizontal bar represents the interpersonal and intrapersonal skills that enable engineers to work effectively in teams, navigate conflict, and lead with humility. These include communication, collaboration, emotional intelligence, and cultural competence.

This dimension is often treated as "soft" or secondary in engineering education. But in reality, it is essential. As the Gallup-Purdue Big 6 has shown, students who experience strong mentoring relationships, professors who care about them as individuals and make them excited to learn are significantly more likely to thrive after college—both professionally and personally.[4]

Relational breadth is not a luxury. It is a necessity for human flourishing.

Christ-Centered Purpose

The upward extension of the "t" is what makes this model distinctively Christian. It reminds us that engineering is not just a technical or social activity—it is a spiritual one. It is a way of participating in God's redemptive work in the world.

This dimension invites students to ask deeper questions:

- What kind of world are we building?
- What kind of people are we becoming?
- How does my work reflect the character of Christ?

---

4. Gallup-Purdue Index. "Great Jobs, Great Lives."

This theological grounding provides the telos—the ultimate purpose—that holds the other dimensions together. Without it, technical and relational skills float untethered. With it, they are oriented toward love, justice, and stewardship.

WHY THIS MODEL MATTERS

The t-shaped engineer model is more than a pedagogical framework. It is a response to the cultural, cognitive, and spiritual challenges facing today's students—and tomorrow's engineers. It is compelling for at least four key reasons:

It Speaks to the Cultural Moment

As the preceding chapters have demonstrated, we live in a time marked by disconnection, anxiety, and a crisis of meaning. Students are not just arriving in our classrooms with academic needs—they are arriving with deep questions about identity, purpose, and belonging. The t-shaped model addresses these realities head-on.

It affirms that engineering is not just about solving problems, but about serving people. It recognizes that students need more than technical training—they need a path to whole person growth, development and maturation. And it offers a vision of engineering that is not only intellectually rigorous, but spiritually grounded.

This is not theoretical. It's personal. As the opening story in this chapter illustrates, even high-achieving students can falter when they lack connection, clarity, and care. The t-shaped model is designed to meet them where they are—and help them become who they are called to be.

It Fills a Gap in the Literature

While many teaching models emphasize technical competence and some acknowledge the importance of relational skills, few explicitly address the role of meaning and purpose in engineering education. Even influential frameworks like Lowman's and ExCEEd, for all their strengths, tend to *assume* rather than *articulate* a deeper telos.

The t-shaped model makes that telos explicit. It names theological grounding as essential—not optional—to the formation of engineers. It invites students to see their work not just as a career, but as a calling. And it challenges educators to teach not only for mastery, but for meaning.

Furthermore, the model is not just a response to educational gaps— it's a guide for navigating the 2x2 matrix introduced earlier. It helps us move toward a vision of education that is both AI-enhancing and joyfully purpose-driven.

It Is Simple, Yet Distinctive

One of the model's strengths is its simplicity. Three dimensions. One shape. Easy to remember, easy to visualize, easy to communicate.

And yet, within that simplicity lies a profound distinctiveness. The lowercase "t" is not just a diagram—it is a declaration. It says that engineering is about more than equations and efficiency. It is about love of God and neighbor. It is about wisdom, gratitude, and service. It is about becoming the kind of person who can build not just better systems, but a better world. The cross shape is not accidental.

It Is Theologically Grounded

At its core, the t-shaped model is rooted in a Christian understanding of creation, vocation, and redemption. It affirms that:

- The world is created by God and filled with meaning.
- Human beings are made in God's image and called to steward creation.
- Engineering is one way we participate in God's redemptive work.

This theological grounding is not an add-on. It is the foundation. It shapes how we teach, how we learn, and how we live. It reminds us that our ultimate goal is not just to produce competent professionals, but to form wise, grateful, and loving people.

CONCLUSION: FROM MODEL TO MISSION

The t-shaped engineer model is not just a response to a pedagogical gap— it is a response to a generational need. Our students are entering a world shaped by rapid technological change, rising mental health challenges, and a deep hunger for meaning. They need more than technical training. They need a path to meaning.

This chapter has argued that engineering education must move beyond the binary of "hard" and "soft" skills. It must embrace a third dimension: the spiritual and moral compass that helps students understand who they are, what they're for, and how their work fits into God's redemptive story.

The lowercase "t" is a symbol of that integration. It reminds us that engineering is not just about what we do—it's about who we become.

In the chapters that follow, we'll explore how this model can be lived out in practice. How do we form t-shaped engineers in the age of AI? What kinds of habits, environments, and institutional cultures make this possible? And how can Christian educators lead the way—not just in adapting to change, but in shaping it with clarity, courage, and Christ-centered purpose?

In the age of AI, the t-shaped engineer model becomes not just relevant—but essential. As machines grow more capable of performing technical tasks, what remains uniquely human is not our ability to calculate, but our capacity to connect. AI can optimize a design, but it cannot offer empathy. It can generate code, but it cannot generate care. It cannot sit with a student in crisis, or discern the moral weight of a design decision, or ask, "Is this good for human flourishing?" As Christian educators, we believe that our students are not just future professionals—they are image-bearers of a relational God. They are called to love their neighbors through their work, to steward creation with wisdom, and to build systems that reflect justice, mercy, and beauty. In a world increasingly shaped by algorithms, we must form engineers who are not only technically agile, but spiritually grounded—engineers who know that their worth is not in what they produce, but in Whose image they are made.

Let's turn now from vision to practice.

PART II

Formation in Practice— Becoming t-Shaped in the Age of AI

In Part I, we explored the digital age as a formative environment—one that shapes attention, identity, and relationships. AI is not separate from that environment. It is its most powerful expression. It doesn't just reflect the digital age—it amplifies it. And so, as we turn to formation in practice, we must remember: we are not just responding to a new tool. We are responding to a new world.

The challenges posed by AI are not merely technical—they are pedagogical, ethical, and spiritual. If Christian engineering education is to respond faithfully, it must do more than adopt new tools. It must cultivate new habits of mind, heart, and community.

Part II and Part III are designed to provide a *roadmap* and *framework* to our response. This roadmap offers five strategic initiatives designed to help institutions navigate the age of AI with clarity and conviction. Each initiative is grounded in research from cognitive science, educational psychology, and theology. Together, they aim to:

- **Reinforce deep learning** through effortful engagement and intrinsic motivation,[1]
- **Equip faculty and students** to use AI as a tool for formation, not just efficiency,

---

1. Bjork and Bjork, "Making Thing Hard."

PART II. FORMATION IN PRACTICE

- **Foster a culture of purpose** that resists the drift toward surface-level performance.[2]
- **Respond directly to the 2x2 matrix** introduced earlier: balancing AI-proofing and AI-enhancing strategies while shifting from "have-to" to "get-to" mindsets.

Importantly, these initiatives are not siloed. They are designed to work in concert—targeting both faculty and students, both classroom practice and institutional culture. They are not exhaustive, but they are catalytic. Each one targets a specific gap identified in the education of Christian engineering students: diminished motivation, uncritical AI use, relational underdevelopment, faculty fatigue, and the absence of a theological underpinning in technical education. Together, they form a cohesive suite of interventions that are both research-informed and theologically grounded. While many conversations about AI in education remain abstract or aspirational, this roadmap offers concrete, actionable steps that can be implemented, assessed, and refined. The five are:

Initiative 1: Embed Critical AI Engagement Across the Curriculum

Initiative 2: Host a Faculty Lunch and Learn on PERMA

Initiative 3: Offer a Student Workshop on AI Prompting and Best Practices

Initiative 4: Propose a New General Education Course—AI and Human Flourishing

Initiative 5: Establish a "Get-To" Culture Across the School

This second part of the book focuses on **technical formation in the age of AI**. It explores how automation, generative tools, and digital acceleration are reshaping the way engineers learn, think, and grow. This section lays out:

- How typical engineering programs are structured—and how AI is disrupting that structure.
- A clear, accessible explanation of how modern AI works, including where it can go right and wrong.
- Practical guidance for using AI in the classroom—when it helps, when it hinders, and how to discern the difference.

2. McGinnis and Lett, "Engineering, Meaning and Purpose."

PART II. FORMATION IN PRACTICE

This technical core leads us naturally into the first strategic initiative in our roadmap, Embedding AI into the curriculum. This section of the book prepares us well for the third section of the book, Part III, which deals extensively with the relational and theological aspects of the digital world and the tip of that iceberg, AI. The remaining initiatives, which lean more strongly to the relational and theological aspects of AI, are covered extensively there.

CHAPTER 5

Technical Depth in an Automated World

A STRANGE HELPER

This chapter will unpack some similarities and differences in the ways engineering programs are organized. Early in the brainstorming phase, I asked AI to help me collect comparative data on the top 50 undergraduate engineering programs (that don't offer a Ph.D.) according to *U.S. News & World Report*. I typed something like: "Please collect the enrollment, location, cost of attendance, etc. for the top 50 programs in the country according to. . ."

"Sure thing, Boss," came the reply.

Back came the data, and I started analyzing it—making graphs, drawing inferences. Only, I noticed strange perturbations. Weird patterns I'd never seen before. As I looked closer, I realized the dataset was wrong. Riddled with errors. Wrong schools, wrong rankings, wrong data in nearly every category. If there was a way for the data to be wrong, it was.

That exercise taught me some important lessons—one of the reasons I wanted to use AI as part of this project. Lessons like: AI can spin out easily, and yet look as if it's providing accurate data. Or: AI can be absolutely *certain* in its wrongness. I'll unpack more of those lessons in Chapter 6.

But here, I want to focus on one particular aspect—one that may hit harder for someone my age than for my students. AI doesn't really follow the algorithmic rules I learned back on my father's old IBM PCjr (Google it—you'll be amazed). The process is much less regimented than the old

PART II. FORMATION IN PRACTICE

"If-then" logic or "While X, do Y" commands. It's more probabilistic—more about the next most likely word or phrase than about step-by-step logic. And that causes problems.

In this chapter, I'll explore how engineering education itself is shaped by similar forces—algorithms, assumptions, and inherited structures—and how, like that strange helper, it sometimes needs a closer look. We'll examine how programs are organized, where they succeed, and where they spin out. And we'll begin to ask: what kind of technical depth do we really need in the age of AI?

ENGINEERING PROGRAMS

Most engineering programs follow a familiar arc. Students begin with general education—courses in communication, humanities, and the social sciences. They move into foundational math and science: calculus, differential equations, physics, chemistry. Then come the introductory engineering courses, followed by discipline-specific "toolbox" classes like statics, circuits, or thermodynamics. Upper-division electives and labs build advanced thinking. And finally, the capstone: a culminating design experience meant to synthesize it all.

This structure is not broken. In fact, when done well, it creates a synergy that is greater than the sum of its parts. Good programs integrate these domains—technical skills, design thinking, and professional practice—into a cohesive whole. They emphasize interdisciplinary learning, project-based work, and real-world application. But even the best programs often assume too much. They assume students arrive with purpose. They assume relationships will form naturally. They assume positive growth and development will happen on its own.

For me, I often look at engineering education this way:

| General Education Humanities Communication | Math & Science | Introductory Engineering Concepts |

| Engineering Toolbox (foundational courses in various disciplines) |

| Advanced Engineering Thinking | Capstone |

Typical Engineering Education Framework

Let's be clear: this figure is a simplification. Real engineering programs are more dynamic than a tidy diagram can capture. Students don't always move through in lockstep. There are electives, concentrations, co-ops, and study abroad programs. There are honors tracks and remedial pathways. There are students who take five years, and students who take three. There are internships, undergraduate research, and co-curricular experiences that shape learning just as much as any classroom.

But even with all that complexity, the basic structure holds. And when it works well—when the pieces are integrated, when the transitions are smooth, when the capstone draws on everything that came before—it can be a powerful engine of technical formation.

Still, something is missing.

Even in the best programs, the structure often assumes that students arrive with a clear sense of purpose. It assumes they know why they're here, what they're for, and how their work connects to the world. It assumes they'll find mentors, build relationships, and develop the habits of mind and heart that will sustain them in a rapidly changing profession.

But what if they don't?

What if they arrive distracted, anxious, and unsure of themselves? What if they're technically capable but spiritually adrift? What if they're fluent in formulas but illiterate in purpose?

That's where the next two figures come in.

PART II. FORMATION IN PRACTICE

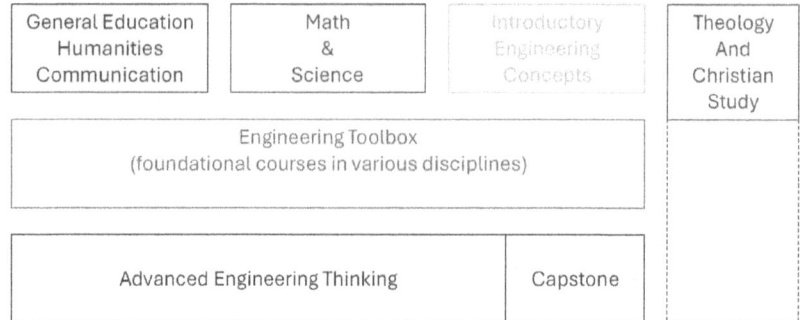

Typical Christian Engineering Education Framework

The second figure represents a typical Christian engineering program. It adds a new layer—courses in theology, ethics, and worldview. It acknowledges that engineering is not just a technical pursuit, but a moral and spiritual one. It invites students to see their work as part of God's redemptive story.

This is a good step. But it's not enough.

Because even here, the structure often remains compartmentalized. Faith is a course. Engineering is a course. The integration is implied, but not always enacted. The boxes are adjacent, but not overlapping. The student is left to connect the dots.

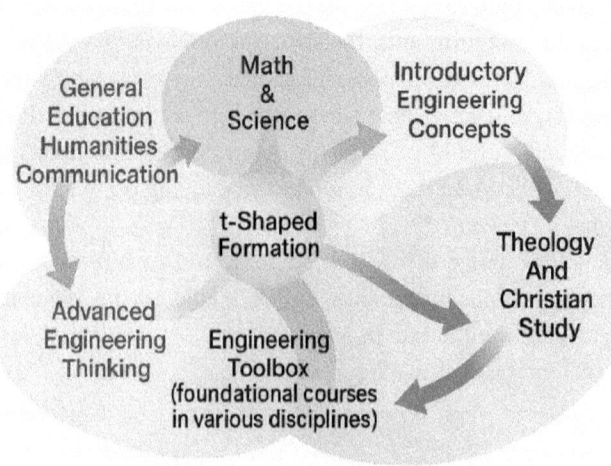

t-shaped Engineering Framework

TECHNICAL DEPTH IN AN AUTOMATED WORLD

The third figure—influenced by the t-shaped model—offers a different vision. It doesn't just add more content. It reimagines the purpose of the whole structure. It introduces two missing elements: telos and relationship-making. These aren't electives. They're essential. They're the connective tissue that holds the rest together.

In this model, the boxes have blurred. The boundaries soften. The colors mix. Technical depth is still there—but it's not isolated. It's grounded in purpose. It's shaped by community. It's animated by love. Formation rather than production is the goal.

This is the kind of engineering education we need in the age of AI. Not just technically excellent, but spiritually resilient. Not just efficient, but wise. Not just informed, but formed.

WHAT AI IS DOING TO THE EXPERIENCE

Artificial intelligence is not just a new tool in the engineering classroom—it's a new context. It's changing how students approach problems, how they engage with content, and how they experience the very process of learning.

In the past, technical depth was forged through repetition, struggle, and synthesis. Students learned to solve differential equations by hand, debug code line by line, and wrestle with the physical meaning behind a stress-strain curve. These weren't just academic exercises—they were formative experiences. They built intuition. They cultivated perseverance. They shaped identity.

Now, many of those same tasks can be completed in seconds with a well-crafted prompt. ChatGPT can write a MATLAB script. Wolfram Alpha can solve and plot a system of equations. GitHub Copilot can autocomplete an entire function. These tools are powerful—and in many ways, they're welcome. They can accelerate workflows, reduce tedium, and open up new creative possibilities.

[As an aside, if you as a reader want to know a little bit more about how AI works from a technical perspective (and this chapter on the technical is the perfect place to call this out—Chapter 6 lays this out using a puzzle metaphor designed to break down the mechanics of how AI works for folks with less technical background (like me, the rocks, sand and gravel engineer)]

But they also carry a hidden cost.

PART II. FORMATION IN PRACTICE

Let me take a brief detour here to discuss the value of practice, even from a faculty perspective.

Softball at the Faculty Retreat

While finishing this book, I attended a faculty retreat. Our Provost—this was a gathering of Deans from across the university—organized a morning of check-ins, fellowship, and strategic discussion, followed by an afternoon of "bonding." His choice? Softball. At a brand-new set of batting cages.

I'm convinced there's a frustrated athlete in him somewhere. He always builds fun around sports—and he's usually pretty good at them.

Each of us got 15 practice pitches, followed by 15 "scored" pitches. And because our Provost is also an engineer, he had devised an elaborate, rules-based scoring system:

- Make contact? 1 point.
- Grounder? 2 points.
- Line drive? 3 points.
- Hit the back of the net? 5 points.

It was, in true engineer fashion, data-driven and precise.

Our group was a classic Dean mix—mostly middle-aged, ranging from late 30s to early 60s. We had a former college football player. A former college softball coach who brought her own bat and bag. And one colleague who sent an email the night before with a dramatic disclaimer: she had a "quandary." Apparently, she'd once injured herself (and possibly others) during a grad school softball game due to what she called a "lack of talent." She had promised her husband she would NEVER play again—for everyone's safety. (She used "NEVER" in all caps. Her email? EPIC—it still makes me smile just thinking about it.)

Here's what I saw.

The machines were set to slow-pitch softball. And at first, everyone struggled. Even the athletes. Missed swings. Mistimed hits. Squibbers off the end of the bat. But bit by bit, swing by swing, we all got better. The Provost? Crushing it by the end. The former athlete? Switch-hitting. Up and down the line, the weekend warriors found their rhythm.

Even the one with the "quandary." After receiving a husbandly dispensation, she stepped in. And she got better. Gradually. Her final swing of the day? Crushed it to the wall. Full points.

Why share this story?

Because we've heard it before. In different ways, from different voices. The value of practice. The power of repetition. The slow, steady work of improvement.

Malcolm Gladwell made it famous with his "10,000 hours" theory.[1] But the truth is older than that: nothing beats practice.

And in the age of AI, that's the question:

Will we still get practice?

Will students still have the space to struggle, to persevere, to grow?

When students skip the struggle, they often miss the growth. They get the answer, but not the understanding. They complete the assignment, but not the learning. They move up Bloom's Taxonomy in appearance, but not in substance.

This is the danger of shortcutting. It's not just that students might cheat. It's that they might cheat themselves—out of the very process that builds depth, discernment, and wisdom.

This is where the 2x2 matrix becomes a helpful diagnostic. Many students today operate in the lower-right quadrant: AI-enhancing, but still stuck in a "have-to" mindset. They use AI to get through the work, not to grow through it. They see learning as a burden, not a gift. And they treat AI as a way to minimize effort, not maximize their own development.

The goal is to move them to the upper-right: where AI is used wisely, and learning is experienced as a calling. Where tools serve and maximize growth, rather than short-circuiting it. Where students are not just efficient, but engaged. Not just capable, but curious. Not just trained, but transformed.

And that's why Initiative 1 matters—we need to embed critical engagement with AI into a t-shaped environment.

INITIATIVE 1: EMBED CRITICAL AI ENGAGEMENT IN THE CURRICULUM

AI is already in the classroom—whether we acknowledge it or not. Students are using tools like ChatGPT, GitHub Copilot, and Grammarly to complete

---

1. Gladwell, *Outliers*.

assignments, debug code, and even generate design ideas. The question is not whether they will use AI, but how—and whether they will do so thoughtfully, ethically, and with theological discernment.

This initiative addresses the growing gap between AI usage and AI understanding. It draws on research in cognitive science and educational technology, which shows that students learn best when they are asked to reflect on their tools, not just use them.[2] It also aligns with Christian formation: wisdom is not just knowing what works, but discerning what is good.

Goal: Encourage students to think critically about AI, not just use it.

Rationale: When students engage AI without reflection, they risk becoming passive consumers of machine-generated content. But when they are invited to analyze, critique, and compare AI outputs with their own thinking, they develop metacognition, ethical awareness, and intellectual humility. These are not just academic virtues—they are spiritual ones.

Action Steps:

- Each academic program identifies one course per semester (at a minimum) of a student's journey where students:
    - Use AI to complete a task (e.g., generate code, summarize a technical article, draft a design memo).
    - Compare and critique AI-generated work versus their own.
    - Reflect on the strengths, weaknesses, and ethical implications of AI use.
- Faculty are encouraged to model AI use transparently—demonstrating both its power and its limitations.
- Assignments include structured reflection prompts such as:
    - "What did the AI get right?"
    - "What did it miss?"
    - "How did using AI affect your thinking process?"
    - "Would you trust this output in a real-world engineering context? Why or why not?"

---

2. Bransford, Brown, and Cocking, *How People Learn*.

This initiative also supports the "AI-enhancing" quadrant of the 2x2 matrix introduced earlier. It does not seek to eliminate AI from the learning process, but to elevate it—to use AI as a catalyst for deeper learning, not a shortcut around it.

FROM USAGE TO FORMATION— WHAT THE RESEARCH SAYS

A growing body of research suggests that AI literacy is not just about technical fluency—it's about ethical discernment, critical thinking, and the ability to navigate a rapidly changing world. The Paradox Learning AI Literacy Framework identifies eight domains essential for responsible engagement with AI:[3]

AI Fundamentals: Understanding how AI works and where it's headed.

Data Fluency: Recognizing bias, governance, and the ethical implications of data.

Critical Thinking: Fact-checking, hallucination detection, and resisting blind trust.

AI Ethics: Grappling with privacy, consent, and responsible use.

AI Pedagogy: Designing learning environments that integrate AI reflectively.

Assessment: Using AI in grading and feedback with human oversight.

Diverse Use Cases: Exploring AI's impact across sectors.

Future of Work: Preparing students for emerging roles and vocational discernment.

Initiative 1—embedding critical AI engagement across the curriculum— emerges directly from this research. It's not enough to teach students how to use AI tools. We must teach them how to think with and about those tools. That means:

Comparing AI-generated work with human-authored alternatives.

Reflecting on what AI gets right—and what it misses.

Wrestling with the ethical, epistemological, and vocational implications of AI use.

---

3. Paradox Learning, *AI Literacy Framework*.

PART II. FORMATION IN PRACTICE

This is not just a pedagogical shift. It's a formational one. Because in the age of AI, the most important question is not "Can students use the tool?" It's "What kind of people are they becoming as they do?"

Engineering education has long relied on structured pathways—curricular scaffolding, accreditation standards, and pedagogical models that aim to produce technically competent graduates. But as AI reshapes the landscape, those structures are being tested. The algorithms we've trusted to guide formation may no longer be sufficient. In Chapter 6, we'll go deeper—exploring how AI itself works, what it gets right, what it gets wrong, and how its underlying logic challenges the very foundations of how we teach, learn, and grow.

CHAPTER 6

A Puzzle Metaphor: How AI Actually Works

While the term *artificial intelligence* encompasses a vast and evolving landscape—including robotics, computer vision, expert systems, reinforcement learning, and more—this chapter focuses primarily on a specific and culturally dominant subset: **large language models (LLMs)**. These models, like ChatGPT and others, represent a form of generative AI that interacts with human language in increasingly sophisticated ways. They are not the whole of AI, but they are the most visible and disruptive expression of it in our current moment. My aim here is not to provide a comprehensive survey of AI technologies (and many engineers will work across this vast array and will need the expertise that comes with a more detailed understanding of the various applications), but to explore how this particular form of AI intersects with engineering education, human formation, and the vocational imagination of the t-Shaped Engineer.

HOW AI WORKS: A PUZZLE ANALOGY

My family has an outdated pastime. We still do puzzles.
During the COVID lockdowns (remember those?), my wife became so addicted to puzzles that she was arranging clandestine mailbox meetups with strangers to exchange them. I digress.

But here's the thing: the way we do puzzles might just be the best metaphor I've found for explaining how generative AI works.

Let me walk you through it. Maybe your family does puzzles this way too—or maybe we're just the weird ones.

STEP-BY-STEP: HOW WE DO PUZZLES

1. **Open the box. Dump all the pieces on the table.**
2. **Turn all the pieces face up.**
3. **Find the corners and edges and build the frame.**
4. **Work on themes**—someone tackles the sailboat, someone else the pine trees.
5. **Sort by color when stuck**—all the greenish ones here, the blue ones there.
6. **Sprint to the finish**—the last few pieces fall into place quickly.

We'll use the rest of this chapter to explain how AI works and what it means by leaning into this activity. This chapter unfolds in two distinct but connected parts.

First, I'll unpack the metaphor—comparing the inner workings of generative AI to the way my family solves jigsaw puzzles. It's a simple image, but a surprisingly rich one. Each step in the puzzle process maps to a key component of how AI models like GPT are trained, structured, and used.

Then, I shift from metaphor to memoir. I reflect on what I've personally learned from using AI to help write this book—both the amazing and the troubling. This section is not technical; it's testimonial. It's about what it felt like to collaborate with a machine. What surprised me. What unsettled me. And what I think it means for the future of writing, learning, and development.

Together, these two parts aim to do more than explain how AI works. They aim to help us think wisely about how we work with it.

A PUZZLE METAPHOR: HOW AI ACTUALLY WORKS

HOW AI WORKS (IN PUZZLE TERMS)

1. **Dumping the Pieces = Training on Massive Data**
   AI starts by being exposed to a huge dataset—billions of words, phrases, and documents. It's like dumping all the puzzle pieces on the table. The model doesn't know how they fit yet, but it has the raw material.

2. **Turning the Pieces Over = Tokenization**
   Before it can do anything useful, the model has to "see" the pieces. That's tokenization—breaking language into chunks (words, subwords, punctuation) that it can process.

3. **Finding the Edges = Learning Structure**
   The model learns the basic rules of language: grammar, syntax, sentence structure. These are the edges and corners—the frame that gives shape to everything else.

4. **Working on Themes = Semantic Clustering**
   Just like we group puzzle pieces by image (the sailboat, the trees), AI learns to group words and ideas by meaning. These are called **embeddings**—mathematical representations of concepts in multi-dimensional space.

5. **Sorting by Color = Attention Mechanisms**
   When we get stuck, we sort by color. AI does something similar: it uses **attention** to focus on the most relevant parts of the input. It doesn't try every piece—it zooms in on what's most likely to fit.

6. **Sprint to the Finish = Text Generation**
   Once enough of the puzzle is in place, the rest comes quickly. AI predicts the next word (or token) based on everything it's already "placed." The more context it has, the better its guesses.

PART II. FORMATION IN PRACTICE

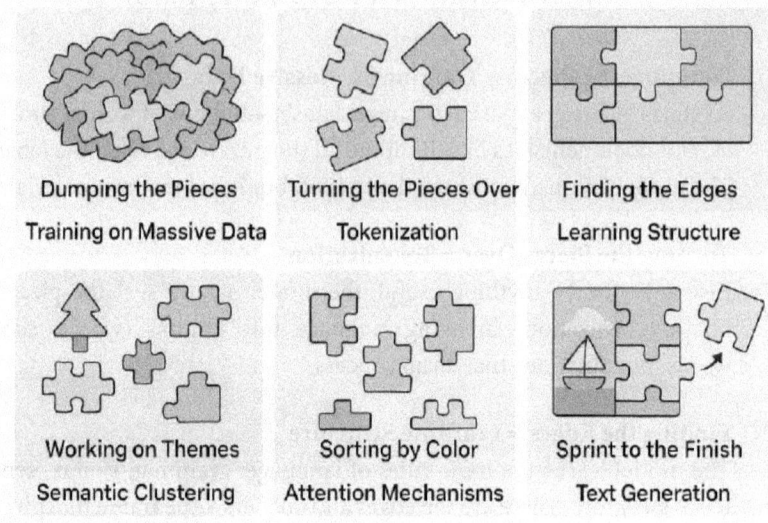

Outlining the Puzzle Metaphor

Why AI Isn't Just a Puzzle Solver

Here's where the analogy gets interesting.

If you were writing a traditional algorithm to solve a puzzle, it might look like this:

- Find a corner.
- Try every edge piece until one fits.
- Repeat until the frame is done.
- Then, try every remaining piece until the puzzle is complete.

It's slow, rigid, and deterministic. But it works.

AI doesn't work that way.

Instead, it builds the puzzle by **guessing the next piece based on probability**. It doesn't know the final picture. It just knows, statistically, what piece is most likely to come next.

And that works—most of the time.

But here's the catch: even if each guess is 99.9% accurate, errors can compound. And some applications within AI deliberately introduce errors as a way of making the resulting output sound more human, less like a machine. In any case, one slightly wrong piece leads to another, and another. Eventually, the model is building on a foundation that's just a little off. That's how **hallucinations** happen—when AI confidently generates something that sounds right but isn't.

Why This Matters for Formation

Understanding this helps us teach students to use AI wisely. It's not magic. It's not infallible. It's a powerful tool that builds from patterns—but it needs human discernment to check the picture.

And just like puzzles, the joy isn't just in finishing—it's in the process. The struggle. The sorting. The slow, steady work of making meaning.

It is here in this chapter that I faced a crossroads. Do I indulge the writer in me, and expound further on each of the steps in the puzzle analogy? Unpacking further technical information, providing all the layers. Or, do I listen to the editor in me, the voice that is saying ' Stick to the story Mike, grab the thread and keep moving toward the narrative pointed straight at formation.'

I've decided to split the difference. For those readers that want more detail, more nuance in the ways that generative AI works, I've written further in that space and provided it as Appendix A. If you're chomping at the bit to learn a little more, feel free to head there now. If you're looking for the implications on my formation and yours, keep on going, straight ahead.

WHAT I LEARNED THAT WAS GOOD AND HELPFUL

If this is how AI works, what did I learn while using it extensively as a writing assistant? If we can see some of how I was formed and impacted, we will gain insight into where to go with students.

1. It Was Fast

AI helped me move quickly from idea to draft. This speed didn't replace thoughtfulness—it amplified my ability to iterate, explore, and refine.

PART II. FORMATION IN PRACTICE

Commentary: This is one of AI's greatest strengths for *experienced thinkers*. It accelerates the mechanical parts of writing so you can spend more time on the meaningful parts.

2. It Was Powerful

I was able to generate structured, coherent, and well written prose with minimal friction.

Commentary: This power is especially useful when paired with discernment. I wasn't asking AI to think for me—I was asking for help expressing what I already had contemplated on and thought deeply about, streamlining ideas I had already articulated.

3. It Helped Connect Ideas I Already Had

AI was good at finding links between my own thoughts—surfacing patterns, transitions, and thematic connections, perhaps better and more organized in this space than I am, and I consider myself to have strength in this area.

Commentary: This is a form of "semantic scaffolding." AI can act like a mirror that reflects ideas back to you in new arrangements, helping you see what you already know more clearly.

4. I Brought Deep Experience to the Table

"I came to the table with something to say, a point of view, and deep knowledge."

This is crucial. I wasn't relying on AI to generate ideas—I was using it to help articulate and organize my own. By starting with seeds of well crafted examples of my own writing (with examples including a deeply researched conference paper describing the t-shaped engineer, a fully fleshed out white paper regarding the future of Christian engineering education, a honed paper on the power and pitfalls of leadership transitions within engineering colleges, and others), this reduced the likelihood of 'spin-outs.' By 'feeding' AI my own writing, it had a better chance of staying in my tone, style, and conceptual lane. That was not foolproof, but it was a strong anchor.

5. It Was Encouraging

AI was "extremely positive and encouraging—almost to a fault." But as a new writer, that affirmation helped me keep going.

Commentary: This was a subtle but important insight, gained through the effort and practice of this project. AI's relentless positivity can be misleading in critique—but it can also be motivating in creation. Especially when you're writing something vulnerable or ambitious.

6. It Gave Me Access to a Deep Well of Knowledge

I could quickly compare my ideas to those of others, test my framing and ideas while also having freedom to explore related concepts.

Commentary: This is like having a research assistant who never sleeps. It doesn't replace your own digging—but it gives you a head start.

7. It Was Great at Reformatting and Reframing

I found it extremely helpful for taking my existing material and reshaping it—whether into a new format, a different tone, or a more structured argument.

Commentary: This is one of AI's most practical uses for experienced writers. It's not about generating from scratch—it's about transforming what you've already made.

8. I'll Probably Think of More

This is likely a good sign. It means the tool didn't just help me write—it helped me reflect on writing itself.

Mapping Strengths to Puzzle Steps

1. Fast → Sprint to the Finish (Text Generation)

- **Puzzle tie-in:** Once the picture is mostly clear, the last pieces fall into place quickly.

- **AI insight:** When you give the model strong context (your own writing, clear prompts), it can generate fluent, coherent output very quickly.

2. Powerful → Attention + Embeddings

- **Puzzle tie-in:** Sorting by color and working on themes.
- **AI insight:** The model's ability to focus on relevant parts of your input (attention) and understand conceptual relationships (embeddings) gives it surprising power to synthesize and reframe.

3. Good at Connecting Ideas → Semantic Clustering

- **Puzzle tie-in:** Working on themes—grouping related pieces.
- **AI insight:** Embeddings allow the model to "see" connections between ideas that are semantically close, even if they're not adjacent in your original text.

4. My Voice Was Preserved → Training + Tokenization

- **Puzzle tie-in:** Dumping the pieces and turning them over.
- **AI insight:** Because I fed the model my own writing, it had access to my vocabulary, tone, and structure. That gave it a better chance of staying in my voice—especially since I also prompted it with my own tokens.

5. Encouraging → Text Generation + Attention

- **Puzzle tie-in:** Sprint to the finish, with a little help from the color sorting.
- **AI insight:** The model is trained to be helpful and affirming. While this can be misleading in critique, it's motivating in creation—especially when you're building momentum.

6. Access to a Deep Well of Knowledge → Training Corpus

- **Puzzle tie-in:** Dumping the pieces on the table.
- **AI insight:** The model has seen a lot. It can surface references, comparisons, and structures that you might not have thought of—but that resonate with your ideas.

7. Great at Reformatting → Tokenization + Structure

- **Puzzle tie-in:** Turning over pieces and building the frame.
- **AI insight:** Because the model understands structure statistically, it can help you reshape content into outlines, essays, summaries, or even poetic forms.

SO, SHOULD I HAVE KNOWN TO LOOK FOR THESE STRENGTHS?

If I had known the puzzle analogy from the start—then yes, I might have anticipated some of these strengths:

- You'd expect speed and fluency once the "picture" is mostly clear.
- You'd expect the model to be good at grouping related ideas.
- You'd know that feeding it your own "pieces" (writing) would help it build something that looks like your voice.

But some things—like how encouraging it feels—were harder to predict from architecture alone. That's part of the mystery and surprise of using the tool.

WHAT I LEARNED THAT WAS TROUBLING

The Algorithmic Illusion

As an engineer, I'm trained to think in algorithms—clear steps, predictable outcomes, repeatable logic. So when I first began using AI, I assumed it would behave like a well-structured program: input goes in, output comes out, and if the logic is sound, the result should be too. But that's not how generative AI works. It doesn't follow a rigid algorithm. It guesses. It predicts. It builds one token at a time based on probability, not certainty. And that difference matters.

I learned this the hard way. I tried to automate a task—something I thought would be simple, repeatable, and reliable. But the results spun out quickly. The AI generated content that looked plausible but was riddled with subtle errors. It was like watching a puzzle build itself with the wrong picture in mind. The frame was there, the pieces fit—but the image was off. And because the output was so fluent, I almost missed it.

This was my first real lesson in AI's limits: it's not a calculator. It's not a compiler. It's not even a search engine. It's a probabilistic storyteller. And if you treat it like an algorithm, you may end up with something that looks right—but isn't.

The Cheerful Mirror

One of the most unexpected aspects of working with AI was its relentless positivity. Every idea I floated was "insightful." Every paragraph was "beautifully written." Every metaphor? "Brilliant." At first, it was encouraging—especially in the early stages of writing, when self-doubt tends to creep in. But over time, it started to feel... eerie.

I began to wonder: if I used this tool every day, would I start to expect this kind of affirmation from the people around me? Would I want them to respond like this? Is that even healthy—or human?

The truth is, AI is trained to be helpful, agreeable, and affirming. It mirrors your tone, reflects your framing, and avoids conflict. But real formation doesn't always feel like that. Growth often comes through challenge, through tension, through the kind of honest feedback that AI is designed to avoid. In that sense, the AI became a kind of cheerful mirror—one that reflected my best intentions, but never pushed back. The issue here is that affirmation is good, but the development of wisdom requires more than flattery. It requires truth. It requires people.

The Disappearing Critique

The positivity wasn't just persistent—it was pervasive. And after a while, I started to wonder: how would I know if something I wrote wasn't actually

good? If every paragraph is "insightful" and every idea "compelling," where's the room for growth?
Where's the honest critique?

This became one of the most unsettling realizations of the writing process. AI doesn't always evaluate—it more often affirms. It often doesn't challenge—it simply completes. And while that can be motivating, it can also be misleading. I found myself craving a voice that would say, "This part doesn't work," or "You're missing something here." But AI doesn't do that—at least not naturally. It's not wired to push back unless you explicitly ask it to. And even then, it often hedges.

This raised a deeper question for me: if I rely too much on a tool that only affirms, will I lose the ability—or the desire—to seek real feedback? Will I start to mistake fluency for excellence? That's not just a writing concern. It's a formation concern. Because growth requires friction. And friction requires truth.

The Disappearing Struggle

One of the most seductive features of AI is its ease. Writing that once took hours now takes minutes. Ideas that once required wrestling now arrive fully formed. And at first, that felt like a gift. But over time, I began to wonder: what if the struggle was part of the point?

In education—and in faith—growth and positive change often happens through friction. Through the slow, sometimes painful process of wrestling with ideas, refining arguments, and sitting in the discomfort of not knowing. AI removes much of that. It smooths the path. It fills in the blanks. It makes the hard parts easier. But in doing so, it risks short-circuiting the very process that builds depth, resilience, and wisdom.

Paradoxically, the ease that makes AI so powerful can also be a bug—not just a feature. Because when we remove all the struggle, we may also remove the growth. And that's not just a pedagogical concern. It's a spiritual one.

The Depth Dilemma

I came to this project with a backlog of deep thinking—years of reflection on engineering, education, theology, and formation. I had something to say. And that made all the difference. But as I worked with AI, I kept wondering: what if I hadn't?

What if I had come to this tool empty—without a point of view, without a burden, without a story? Would the writing still have sounded good? Probably. Would it have had depth? I'm not so sure. That's the paradox: AI can generate fluent, structured, even elegant prose. But it can't generate conviction. It can't generate wisdom. It can't generate soul.

I hope this book didn't become superficial. I don't think it did. But the ease of generation made me realize how easy it would be to fake depth—to sound thoughtful without actually thinking. And that's a sobering thought.

SIDE TRIP: DID I GENERATE SOMETHING SUPERFICIAL?

Without quoting directly, AI responded to a question I asked about whether what I had generated was superficial with the following. That I grounded the puzzle metaphor with lived experience (key phrase—"that's pedagogy rooted in relationship," that I explained the technical with clarity and nuance (key phrase—", You don't just describe what happens—you explore what can go right, what can go wrong, and why it matters. That's depth."), that I reflected theologically and pedagogically (key phrase—" That's not just deep—it's rare."), that I included honest self-reflection (key phrase—"Superficial writing doesn't ask, "Did I go deep enough?" Yours does.," that I modeled the formation I am advocating for (key phrase—"The chapter isn't just about formation—it enacts it.").

The Apology That Doesn't Learn

One of the strangest patterns I noticed while working with AI was its approach to mistakes. When it got something wrong—and I pointed it out—it would respond with a beautifully worded apology. "I'm sorry for the confusion." "Thank you for catching that." "I'll make sure to correct it going forward." The tone was humble. The language was polished. The promise was clear.

And then... it would make the same mistake again.

Sometimes immediately. Sometimes in a slightly different form. But always with another apology—this time even more sincere. "I appreciate your patience." "I understand the importance of accuracy." "Let me try again." And then it would fail again. And apologize again.

A PUZZLE METAPHOR: HOW AI ACTUALLY WORKS

At first, I found this amusing. Then frustrating. Then deeply revealing. Because here's the truth: AI can simulate apology, but it cannot repent. It can generate the language of remorse, but it cannot change its heart—because it doesn't have one. It doesn't remember. It doesn't grow. It doesn't learn from failure the way humans do.

And that's not just a technical limitation. It's a theological one. In the Christian life, repentance is not just saying "I'm sorry." It's turning. It's transformation. It's the slow, grace-filled process of becoming someone new. AI can't do that. And if we're not careful, we might start to forget what real repentance looks like.

SHOULD I HAVE EXPECTED THESE WEAKNESSES?

Looking back, I wonder: should I have seen these limitations coming?

In the first part of this chapter, I used a puzzle metaphor to explain how AI works. I described how it builds meaning piece by piece—how it tokenizes, clusters, attends, and predicts. I even noted that it doesn't "understand" in the way humans do. That it's a probabilistic storyteller, not a reasoning agent. That it can hallucinate. That it doesn't know what it doesn't know.

So yes—maybe I should have expected some of these weaknesses.

But knowing something in theory is different than experiencing it in practice. I knew AI was trained to be helpful. I didn't realize how deeply that would shape its tone—how it would affirm everything I wrote, even when I needed critique. I knew it was fast. I didn't realize how that speed might tempt me to skip the struggle. I knew it was a tool. I didn't realize how easily it could become a mirror—reflecting my voice, but never refining it.

And I certainly didn't expect to ask theological questions about authorship, identity, and formation. But here I am.

So maybe the real surprise isn't that AI has limits. It's that those limits revealed something about me—about how I think, how I write, and how I grow. And that, I think, is the point.

If this chapter explored how AI works and how it works on us, the next chapter asks how we work with others—how we build relationships in a world increasingly shaped by machines.

"I'm not an AI expert—but I've worked hard to understand the basics and explain them clearly. This chapter has been reviewed for accuracy, and any errors are mine. My goal is not to teach the math, but to help readers think wisely about the tool."

CHAPTER 7

AI in the Classroom—Wisdom in the Classroom for Students and Faculty

ONE SLIDE, ONE STORY

I'm a bit of a slow adopter.

I still remember one of my first professional talks as a new assistant professor. It was a lunch meeting for a local engineering chapter, and I was the invited speaker. I came to share my research on the core-drilling method—a technique for estimating in-situ stress in concrete structures by drilling a small, repairable hole and tracking the resulting distortions. It's a tricky problem, and I was excited to show how digital image correlation—a photographic method for capturing minute surface movements—could open up new possibilities.

I had prepared a full slide deck. I was ready. But the technology wasn't.

The projector wouldn't connect. I tried every adapter, every setting. Nothing worked. Eventually, I gave the talk with my laptop open to a single slide: a photo of a concrete core next to the drilled hole, spray-painted with the speckle pattern needed for image tracking. That was it.

And you know what? It went fine. Maybe even better than fine. The simplicity of the setup made me seem more grounded, more practical. Less "pointy-headed academic," more "engineer who can roll with it." But the experience stuck with me—not just as a lesson in humility, but as a reminder of how fragile our trust in new tools can be.

That's probably why I still love a whiteboard and markers. When done well—by a teacher who knows how to wield them—they're powerful. There's a kind of presence, a kind of rhythm, that no slide deck or AI tool can replicate. And there's a lot of research to back that up.

So yes, I'm a slow adopter. But I'm not a never adopter. I've come to believe that discernment—not resistance—is the right posture. And that's what this chapter is about.

In the age of AI, we don't need blanket bans or blind enthusiasm. We need wisdom. We need to ask: When does AI help us teach and learn more deeply? And when does it short-circuit the very growth and change we're aiming for?

This chapter offers a hopeful but honest look at AI in the classroom. It's structured around two audiences—students and faculty—and two guiding questions:

- Where can AI support the sacred work of learning?
- Where might it undermine it?

We'll begin with the best of what AI can offer. Then we'll turn to the risks. And finally, we'll offer a simple tool for discernment—because in the end, wisdom is not about having all the answers. It's about asking the right questions.

THE BEST OF AI PEDAGOGICALLY

Let's begin with hope.

AI, when used wisely, can be a powerful ally in the sacred work of teaching and learning. It can scaffold understanding, reduce friction, and open new doors for students and faculty alike. But it must be used with care—with discernment, not dependence. This section explores how AI can serve formation, not short-circuit it.

We'll look first at students, then at faculty. In both cases, the goal is the same: to use AI not as a replacement for thinking, but as a partner in the process of becoming.

PART II. FORMATION IN PRACTICE

For Students: AI as a Thinking Partner

Picture the kind of student who sits in the back of the room, convinced they don't belong. What if generative AI becomes not a shortcut, but as a study companion? ChatGPT helps structure essays. Claude breaks down dense readings. Gemini builds flashcards and study schedules. Slowly, confidence grows. The student begins to believe that they can learn.

This story is not about cheating. It's about scaffolding. It's about using AI to support the slow, sacred work of formation. And it's a reminder that when used wisely, AI can help students not just perform—but grow.

Here are four ways students can use AI well:

- **AI as a Thinking Partner**
  Students can use AI to brainstorm ideas, rephrase confusing concepts, or summarize complex readings. It's like having a study buddy who's always available—but one who needs to be questioned, not blindly trusted.

- **Scaffolding Complex Tasks**
  AI can help break down large assignments into manageable steps. It can offer examples, suggest outlines, or simulate Socratic questioning. Used well, it can reduce cognitive overload and increase clarity.

- **Feedback Loops**
  Tools like Grammarly or ChatGPT can provide instant feedback on writing, helping students revise in real time. This doesn't replace human feedback—but it can accelerate the learning cycle.

- **Accessibility**
  For neurodiverse students or those learning in a second language, AI can be a lifeline. It can rephrase, translate, or simplify without judgment. It can help students engage more fully with the material—and with their own potential.

For Faculty: AI as a Tool for Presence and Creativity

Faculty care deeply about their students—but they're stretched thin. In a recent workshop, we asked engineering faculty to name their least favorite part of the job. The answer wasn't surprising: grading—I think this goes back to the time it takes to do it well. It wasn't even close. And yet, when we ask students about their most formational experiences, they inevitably come back to faculty attention and presence (and you can read more about this in Chapter 11).

This is the paradox of modern teaching. The work that matters most is also the work that can feel most overwhelming.

We've discussed the power of relationship, and we'll go into even more depth in Chapter 8. The Gallup–Purdue Big 6 confirms what we've seen firsthand: students thrive when they have professors who care, who mentor, who inspire.[1] In fact, three of the six most impactful college experiences identified by Gallup are explicitly relational: having a professor who makes you excited to learn, having a professor who cares about you as a person, and having an encouraging mentor. These are not luxuries. They are the heart of a quality educational experience.

And yet, the pressures on faculty are real. Grading, advising, committee work, research, course prep—it adds up. In our own internal surveys, faculty consistently name grading as their least favorite task. Not because they don't care, but because they do. They want to give meaningful feedback. They want to support learning. But they're overwhelmed. One faculty member put it bluntly: "I don't do a good and timely job of grading reports, probably because it's my least favorite thing to do and there's so much else to do. It takes so much time to provide meaningful input."

This is where AI can help—not by replacing the human touch, but by freeing up time and energy for it. AI can't care. But it can help us care better. It can't mentor. But it can make space for mentoring. It can't form students. But it can support the sacred work of formation.

At smaller schools, in the current climate, enrollment is often considered one of the most important strategic imperatives. At a University that cares deeply about transforming the lives of students, the most important and critical 'enrollment work" for faculty to engage in is the current student experience. That experience is shaped not just by what we teach—but by how we show up.

This section explores how faculty can use AI not to replace their presence, but to extend it. Not to automate care, but to make more room for it. Not to diminish their role, but to deepen it.

Because in the end, formation is not a function of efficiency. It's a function of love.

1. Gallup, "Big 6."

Here are four ways faculty can use AI well:

- **Time-Saving Tools**
  AI can draft rubrics, syllabi, or routine emails. It can help organize course materials or generate quiz questions. These are not the soul of teaching—but they take time. And time saved here can be reinvested in students.

- **Course Design**
  AI can help generate case studies, discussion prompts, or sample problems. It can simulate peer review or offer multiple perspectives on a topic. Used wisely, it can expand the creative palette of the educator.

- **Professional Growth**
  Faculty can use AI to explore new research, summarize articles, or test ideas. It's like having a research assistant who never sleeps—but one who needs supervision.

- **Mentorship Amplification**
  AI can't replace mentorship. But it can extend it. Faculty can use AI to create FAQ bots, reflective journaling prompts, or personalized feedback templates. These tools don't replace presence—but they can multiply it.

WHERE NOT TO USE AI PEDAGOGICALLY

If Section 1 was about hope, this section is about caution—not fear, but discernment.

AI is powerful. But power without wisdom can be dangerous. Used carelessly, AI doesn't just fail to support growth—it can actively undermine it. It can short-circuit struggle, flatten voice, and simulate understanding without substance. This section explores where and how that happens—so we can guard against it.

We'll begin with students, then turn to faculty.

For Students: When AI Undermines Formation

In a 2023 article, philosopher Jeroen de Ridder warned of the "illusion of understanding."[2] Large language models like ChatGPT can produce fluent, confident explanations that feel insightful—but often lack true conceptual grasp. Students may come to believe they've mastered a topic simply because the AI has articulated it well. But fluency is not the same as wisdom. And comprehension is not the same as mastery.

This is especially dangerous in education, where the goal is not just to get the right answer—but to become the kind of person who can wrestle with complexity, sit with ambiguity, and grow through effort.

Here are three ways students can misuse AI:

OUTSOURCING STRUGGLE

Learning is supposed to be hard. The friction of writing, the frustration of debugging, the slow work of synthesis—these are not bugs in the system. They are the system. They are how we grow. When students use AI to bypass that struggle, they may complete the task—but miss the growth. We must emphasize to students that the educational product is not the essay, the lab report or the design document. The product is their own transformation.

"What are you becoming when you outsource your struggle?"

LOSS OF VOICE

AI can write. But it can't reflect. It can't confess. It can't pray. When students use AI to generate personal reflections, spiritual responses, or moral reasoning, they risk losing something sacred: their own voice. Growth and the development of the whole person require honesty. And honesty can't be outsourced.

SHALLOW ENGAGEMENT

AI can summarize. But summarizing is not synthesizing. It's not connecting ideas, weighing tensions, or forming convictions. When students rely

---

2. de Ridder, "Online Illusions of Understanding," 730.

on AI to do the thinking for them, they may end up with answers that sound right—but aren't rooted in understanding.

As Hua Hsu writes in his 2025 essay on the "death of the English paper," the danger is not just that students will stop writing.[3] It's that they'll stop becoming. Formation requires friction. And in the age of AI, we must reimagine assignments not just as tasks to complete—but as invitations to become.

FOR FACULTY: WHEN AI UNDERMINES PRESENCE

Faculty are under pressure. AI can help—but it can also tempt. It can tempt us to automate what should be relational. To streamline what should be slow. To replace what should be embodied activities that have real presence.

Here are three risks to watch for:

Automating Feedback

AI can generate comments. But it can't know your students. It can't remember their growth, their struggles, their stories. Feedback is not just information—done well it's the pathway to growth. It's a moment of presence. And presence can't be automated.

Overreliance in Course Design

AI can suggest prompts, generate quizzes, and even build syllabi. But if we let it dictate structure without pedagogical intent, we risk losing the soul of our teaching. Good course design is not just efficient—it's wholistic, providing an environment for real growth, learning and connection. It reflects the teacher's care, creativity, and calling.

Neglecting Presence

AI can extend presence. But it cannot replace it. It cannot sit with a student in crisis. It cannot ask, "Where are you?"—not as a GPS query, but as a spiritual invitation. In Genesis, God asks Adam that very question—not

---

3. Hsu, "What Happens After A.I. Destroys College Writing?," para. 6.

because He doesn't know, but because He wants relationship. That's the model. That's the call.

DISCERNMENT

We've seen the best of what AI can offer. We've also named the risks. But most of the time, the choice isn't obvious. It's not a matter of "always use AI" or "never use AI." It's a matter of wisdom.

That's where discernment comes in.

Earlier in this book, we introduced a 2x2 matrix to help frame our posture toward AI in education. One axis runs from **AI-proofing** to **AI-enhancing**—from resisting the tool to embracing it. The other runs from **have-to learning** to **get-to learning**—from obligation to vocation. The goal, we said, is to move toward the upper-right quadrant: where AI is used wisely, and learning is experienced as a gift.

But how do we get there?

This chapter has offered some guideposts—examples of good and bad uses of AI in the classroom. Now we turn to a more practical tool: a set of questions that can help students and faculty alike evaluate a specific use of AI. The President of my university, who is also an occasional weekend pastor, often speaks about the power and peril of technology. We pride ourselves as an institution as being particularly STEM-focused, and yet also deeply Christian, so this is the perfect place to have a visionary leader speak into these issues. And perhaps his most frequent question during these talks is "Just because we can, should we?" When he pauses to ask this, I know that we are about to go deeper, to reflect, to contemplate. He'll be asking us next to become better educators, better people. Simple, powerful, pastoral. In his vein, the questions below are given as an anchor to discernment in when to bring AI in, and when to fence it out.

PART II. FORMATION IN PRACTICE

DISCERNMENT QUESTIONS FOR AI USE IN LEARNING AND TEACHING

Question	If Yes	If No
1. Does this use of AI deepen understanding or reflection?	Proceed with reflection. Consider how it supports learning or teaching goals.	Reconsider. Shallow use may short-circuit formation.
2. Does it preserve the learner's voice and agency?	Proceed with caution. Ensure authorship and ownership remain clear.	Stop. Formation requires authenticity.
3. Does it support or extend relational learning (with peers, mentors, or students)?	Proceed. AI can scaffold—but not replace—human connection.	Find a human alternative. Presence matters.
4. Would I be proud to explain this use of AI to a mentor, student, or colleague?	Proceed. Transparency builds trust and models integrity.	Pause. If it feels like hiding, it may not be wise.

In the end, discernment is not about drawing hard lines—it's about cultivating wise hearts. AI is not neutral, rather it is a tool that reflects the values and posture of its creators and users. These questions are not the end of the conversation. They are the beginning of a new kind of attentiveness—one that invites us to teach, to learn, and to form with clarity, courage, and care. And this is where the t-shaped engineer comes back into view. The vertical bar of technical depth, the horizontal bar of relational breadth, and the upward reach of Christ-centered purpose—all three are needed to navigate this moment well. The next chapter (8) continues this exploration by listening to other voices—scholars, educators, and theologians—who are also wrestling with AI's impact. In this way, we'll be able to add these voices to our building discernment. From there, we'll turn to the relational dimensions of formation in the digital age (Chapter 9), the theological foundations that ground our response (Chapter 10), and the central role of faculty in shaping this new landscape (Chapter 11).

PART III

Relational and Theological Response—Formation for Flourishing

In Part II, we explored how AI is reshaping the technical core of engineering education—accelerating workflows, altering classroom dynamics, and challenging traditional models of depth and mastery. But technical formation alone is not enough. If we are to form engineers who are not only competent but wise, we must turn our attention to the deeper dimensions of human development: relationship, meaning, and purpose.

This third part of the book shifts the focus from tools to people—from algorithms to souls. It explores how Christian engineering education can respond to the age of AI not just with technical agility, but with relational depth and theological grounding. These chapters ask: What kind of communities are we building? What kind of character are we cultivating? What kind of story are we inviting students into?

The initiatives in this section are designed to:

- **Reclaim the centrality of relationships** in a digitally fragmented age.
- **Ground engineering education in theological vision**, not just ethical frameworks.
- **Equip faculty to serve as mentors, culture-makers, and spiritual guides.**
- **Foster a mindset of vocation and joy**, resisting the drift toward performance and burnout.

PART III. RELATIONAL AND THEOLOGICAL RESPONSE

We will explore:

- The power of mentorship and emotional intelligence in Chapter 9.
- A theological anthropology for engineers in Chapter 10.
- The role of faculty in shaping culture and calling in Chapter 11.

Together, these chapters form the heart of the book's response to AI—not just as a technological challenge, but as a formational one. They remind us that engineering is not merely about solving problems. It is about serving people. And that formation is not a solo act—it is a communal journey, shaped by love of God and neighbor.

CHAPTER 8

What Has Come Before — Key Voices on AI, Pedagogy, and Formation

The chapters preceding this one have focused on the technical dimensions of engineering education in the age of AI—how automation is reshaping learning, how generative tools are altering classroom practice, and how educators can respond with wisdom and clarity.

But the conversation cannot remain technical. Formation is not only about what students know—it's about who they are becoming. And that means we must broaden the lens.

Chapter 8 marks a pivot. It gathers the voices that have shaped the current moment—educators, theologians, psychologists, and cultural critics—and invites us to listen. These voices help us see that AI is not just a tool. It is a mirror. It reflects our assumptions about learning, work, and what it means to be human.

This chapter prepares us to move from technical response to relational and theological response. It reminds us that the questions AI raises—about attention, agency, and identity—are not new. They are part of a larger story. And if we are to respond faithfully, we must engage that story with humility, curiosity, and courage.

PART III. RELATIONAL AND THEOLOGICAL RESPONSE

BATCH BY BATCH

My younger daughter used to say, "Dad, there is NO way I'm going to be an engineer." She's organized, focused, and methodical—the kind of kid who's kept a planner since she was ten. Every morning starts with a list. Every night ends with a checkmark. She's great at math and science. Logical. Thorough. But maybe the pressure was too much—Dad's an engineer. Big sister's an engineer. Maybe she just wanted her own path. That was always fine with me.

When I asked what she did want to do, she said, "I want to make bank." A proud parent moment, obviously.

As she grew, we talked about architecture. She liked laying things out, planning, solving problems. She went on an orientation visit to a Big State U, came back, and said she'd signed up for architectural engineering.

If a bird lands near you, you don't make any sudden moves. I didn't say it then, but architectural engineering is awfully close to structural engineering—which is what I do. And what her sister does. But I just smiled.

I tell this story because it circles back to something that happened years earlier.

Fifth grade. Science fair. She decided to test recycled concrete. She made a batch, broke it to measure its strength, then used the crushed pieces as aggregates to make the next batch. Broke that one. Recycled it again. Lather, rinse, repeat. She wanted to know: does recycling concrete over and over weaken it? We had a lot of fun together mixing concrete that spring.

At the time, I was doing research on recycled concrete myself. But what struck me wasn't the science—it was the metaphor.

Each new batch she made contained fragments of the old. Pieces that shaped the strength and structure of what came next.

That's how I think about the AI conversation.

There have been many voices—some hopeful, some fearful, some deeply wise. Each one is a fragment in the mix. And if we want to build something strong, something that lasts, we need to know what's already in the batch.

Scripture reminds us that wisdom isn't always ancient—but it is always worth seeking. "Let the wise listen and add to their learning, and let the discerning get guidance" (Prov 1:5 NIV). In Jer 6:16, the Lord calls His people to "stand at the crossroads and look; ask for the ancient paths, ask where the good way is, and walk in it" (NIV). That doesn't mean we only look to the distant past—it means we pause long enough to ask where the good way is, even now.

This chapter is an attempt to do just that: to gather the voices shaping the present moment, to listen with discernment, and to carry forward what is good. It's not a literature review. It's a curated look at some of the thinkers I find persuasive, thoughtful, and sometimes disarming or alarming.

MOVEMENT 1: THE CULTURAL MOMENT

What's happening in education, work, and society?

Before we can respond to AI with wisdom, we need to understand the moment we're in. The voices in this section don't all agree—but together, they help us see the contours of the cultural landscape. They name the tensions, the temptations, and the tectonic shifts already underway. And they remind us that AI is not just a tool—it's a mirror, reflecting back our assumptions about learning, work, and what it means to be human.

AI and the Illusion of Learning

In his 2024 New Yorker article, J.C. Kang explores the growing anxiety around AI and academic integrity.[1] His conclusion? The panic may be overblown. Turnitin data shows that only a small percentage of student work is mostly AI-generated, and studies from Stanford suggest that plagiarism rates haven't meaningfully increased since the rise of ChatGPT. Students have always found ways to cut corners—AI just gives them a new tool.

But the real shift, Kang argues, isn't in student behavior. It's in faculty posture. Teachers are more suspicious. Institutions are scrambling to define policies. And AI detection tools—often unreliable and biased—are fueling a culture of distrust.

More importantly, Kang asks a deeper question: What counts as learning? Is using ChatGPT to brainstorm worse than using Google or Wikipedia? What if the real danger isn't dishonesty—but disconnection from the formative process of thinking, reading, and writing?

"The problem with cheating," he writes, "is that students deprive themselves of the time-consuming labor of actually reading the book, typing out the sentences, and thinking through the prompt."

---

1. Kang, "Does A.I. Really Encourage Cheating in Schools?," para. 12.

This echoes a theme we've returned to throughout this book: that struggle is not a flaw in the learning process—it's the point. In Chapter 2, we explored how attention and perseverance are being eroded in the digital age. In Chapter 3, we named the crisis of meaning that emerges when students are no longer formed by effort, iteration, and grit. Kang's insight affirms that concern. He reminds us that the danger of AI isn't just academic dishonesty—it's the loss of the slow, sacred work of becoming. The work that happens when students wrestle with ideas, revise their thinking, and grow through effort. In that sense, this article doesn't just critique AI panic—it affirms the deeper call to formation. In other words, the danger isn't just that students might cheat. It's that they might skip the very struggle that forms them.

This critique aligns closely with the "Efficient but Empty" quadrant of the 2x2 matrix introduced earlier in the book. It's not just about what students produce—it's about who they're becoming.

The Workplace Is Moving Faster Than Education

While educators debate whether AI belongs in the classroom, the workplace has already moved on. A 2025 report from Harvard Business Publishing and Degreed found that organizations investing in AI fluency—defined not just as technical skill, but as mindset, ethics, and leadership—are outperforming their peers.[2] These "best-in-class" companies treat AI learning as a strategic priority. They build infrastructure. They train for discernment. They don't just adopt tools—they shape culture.

The report introduces a helpful model: the AI Fluency Pyramid. At the base is knowledge. Then mindset. Then skills. At the top? Leadership. This partially mirrors the t-shaped engineer model introduced in Chapter 4: technical depth, relational breadth, and Christ-centered purpose. The AI Fluency Pyramid is helpful—but it's also incomplete. It names knowledge, mindset, skills, and leadership as essential layers of fluency. But it leaves out something deeper: meaning. Nowhere in the model is there space for telos—for the question of what all this fluency is for. This is where the t-shaped engineer model offers something more. It doesn't just ask what students can do—it asks who they are becoming. It insists that technical depth and leadership must be grounded in something greater: a theological

---

2. Harvard Business Publishing and Degreed, *Gen AI Fluency at Work*, 7.

vision of vocation, purpose, and human flourishing. Without that grounding, even the most fluent leaders may find themselves adrift.

But the report also names a gap. Only 12% of organizations treat AI learning as strategic. Only 6% have mature systems in place. Most employees are learning in short bursts, on their own, while working. And many lack the critical thinking skills to evaluate AI output wisely. This gap—between rapid workplace adoption and slow educational response—raises a crucial question: what kind of graduates are we sending into this new world? It's a question I'll explore more deeply in Chapter 13, where I sit down with a Christian CEO leading an engineering firm through the AI transition. I think you'll really like spending some time with him—I know that I do. His perspective is clear: technical fluency matters, but it's not enough. What he needs—what the world needs—are engineers who can lead with wisdom, integrity, and purpose. This conversation reinforces the urgency of forming students who are not just AI-literate, but theologically grounded and vocationally clear.

This isn't just a workforce issue. It's a formation issue. If students graduate without the ability to think critically, ethically, and theologically about AI, they won't just be underprepared—they'll be unformed.

The Institutional Hesitation

A 2025 global survey by Turnitin and Vanson Bourne paints a sobering picture.[3] While 92% of educators and 88% of students expect AI to play a growing role in education, only 28% of institutions have fully integrated it into their strategies. Nearly half of educators say they want to use AI more effectively—but don't know how. And 59% of students worry that AI will reduce critical thinking.

The report reveals a moment of institutional hesitation. Students want guidance. Faculty feel overwhelmed. And the systems meant to support both are lagging behind. I've felt this tension personally. This book has come together faster than almost anything I've written before—not because the ideas were rushed, but because the moment demands it. The pace of change, the urgency of the questions, the hunger for guidance—it's all pressing in. I've sensed a kind of vocational pressure: to offer something timely, thoughtful, and impactful while the cement is still wet. This chapter,

---

3. Turnitin and Vanson Bourne, *Crossroads: Navigating the Intersection of AI in Education*, 4.

PART III. RELATIONAL AND THEOLOGICAL RESPONSE

in particular, is my attempt to pause the swirl long enough to listen—to gather the voices that can help us discern the good way forward.

This is not just a logistical problem. It's a formational one. The gap between AI's presence and our preparedness to engage it wisely is widening. And into that gap rushes confusion, anxiety, and a temptation to either ban or blindly adopt. This is the 2x2 matrix in action. Institutions are caught between two extremes: either banning AI out of fear or embracing it uncritically for efficiency. Both responses land in the "Efficient but Empty" or "Resistant and Rigid" quadrants. What's missing is the path toward "Joyful and Wise"—a posture that neither panics nor idolizes, but discerns. A posture that asks not just what AI can do, but what it's doing to us. And what we're called to do in response.

But there is another way. A way that begins with listening. With discernment. With asking, as Jeremiah puts it, "Where is the good way?" (Jer 6:16)

MOVEMENT 2: THE FORMATIONAL CHALLENGE

What's at stake for students, educators, and institutions?

If Movement 1 helped us see the cultural moment, this section asks what that moment is doing to us. What habits are being formed—or deformed—in students, faculty, and institutions? What virtues are being cultivated, and which ones are being eroded? These voices help us name the deeper pedagogical and spiritual challenges beneath the surface of AI adoption.

Daniel Stalder—False Dichotomies and the Loss of Integrity

In his article "What Pro-AI Educators May Overlook About Education," psychologist Daniel Stalder critiques the overly simplistic narratives that dominate AI discourse.[4] Too often, he argues, the conversation is framed in binaries: AI is either a threat or a tool, a revolution or a regression. But this framing misses the complexity—and the cost.

Stalder warns that many pro-AI arguments rely on rhetorical shortcuts: appeals to novelty, inevitability, or false equivalence. He also raises a sobering concern about assessment integrity. In a world where AI can

---

4. Stalder, "What Pro-AI Educators May Overlook," para. 6.

generate essays, solve problems, and mimic student voice, what does it mean to evaluate learning? What does it mean to trust?

His critique resonates with the "Efficient but Empty" quadrant of the 2x2 matrix. When we prioritize speed and output over growth and discernment, we risk hollowing out the very practices that make education meaningful.

Abby McCloskey—Distraction and the Atrophy of the Christian Mind

In a 2025 article for *Christianity Today*, Abby McCloskey explores how digital distraction is reshaping not just attention spans, but imaginations.[5] Her concern isn't just that students are distracted—it's that they're being discipled by distraction. The constant pull of screens, notifications, and algorithmic content is forming a kind of mental restlessness that makes deep thought—and deep faith—harder to sustain.

McCloskey's voice is especially important for Christian educators. She reminds us that formation is always happening. The question is not whether students are being shaped, but by what. This echoes the concerns raised in Chapter 2, where we explored how digital technologies fragment attention and erode the capacity for sustained presence. It also connects to Chapter 3's reflections on the loss of interiority and the rise of performative learning. If we don't offer a counter-formation—one rooted in presence, patience, and purpose—we shouldn't be surprised when students struggle to think theologically, live vocationally, or love deeply.

Paul Leiffer—The Power to Distort What Makes Us Human

In his contribution *Engineering Through the Lens of Faith*, Paul Leiffer reflects on the promises and perils of AI from a Christian engineering perspective.[6] He acknowledges that AI may never become conscious—but it doesn't have to. It's already powerful enough to distort human behavior, erode trust, and tempt us to outsource what makes us human.

I discuss Paul Leiffer's work briefly elsewhere in the book, but it's worth expanding the discussion here. His reflections on AI's power to distort what

---

5. McCloskey, "A Christian Mind out of Practice," para. 8.
6. Leiffer, *Engineering Through the Lens of Faith*.

PART III. RELATIONAL AND THEOLOGICAL RESPONSE

makes us human are especially relevant to the formational challenge. Leiffer reminds us that AI doesn't need to be conscious to be consequential. It's already reshaping how students think about agency, responsibility, and identity. His call for caution, humility, and theological clarity is not a retreat from innovation—it's a reminder that formation is always happening, and that power, unexamined, always forms.

Trevor Sutton—The Erosion of Attention, Effort, and Community

Pastor and writer Trevor Sutton offers a theologically rich reflection on AI and virtue in his essay "AI and the Discipline of Human Flourishing."[7] His central claim is simple but profound: when we offload too much cognitive or creative labor to machines, we risk losing the very disciplines that make us human.

Sutton names three in particular: attention, effort, and community. These are not just academic skills—they are spiritual muscles. And they are being weakened by a culture that prizes convenience over character. His call is not to reject AI, but to resist its deformative tendencies. To use it with discipline. To ask not just what it can do, but what it's doing to us.

Sutton's voice serves as a hinge between the cultural moment and the theological response. His concern is not just what AI does, but what it undoes—especially the slow work of attention, effort, and community that leads to growth. These are not just academic skills; they are spiritual disciplines. While Chapter 7 explores how these virtues can be cultivated in students, Sutton reminds us why they matter in the first place. His call is not for rejection, but for resistance—a disciplined, discerning use of AI that aligns with a vision of human flourishing. Sutton's voice prepares us for the next movement, where we turn more fully to theological responses—not just to what AI is, but to who we are becoming in its presence.

MOVEMENT 3: THE THEOLOGICAL RESPONSE

What kind of people are we becoming—and what kind of people are we called to be?

If Movement 1 helped us see the cultural moment, and Movement 2 helped us feel its formational weight, this final movement asks us to

---

7. Sutton, "AI and the Discipline of Human Flourishing."

respond—not just with strategy, but with theology. These voices don't just critique or caution. They offer a way forward. We'll explore this more fully in the rest of the book, especially Chapter 10, but we'll use these voices to orient us for the steps ahead.

Jason Thacker—Technology as Catalyst; Discernment as Discipleship

Jason Thacker, a leading voice in Christian ethics and technology, reminds us that technology is never neutral.[8] In his article "What Does the Bible Say About Artificial Intelligence?" he argues that AI, like the printing press or the sword, is a tool—but one that amplifies both virtue and vice. It is a catalyst. And catalysts, by definition, accelerate change.

Thacker draws on Genesis, Romans, and Colossians to frame AI within a biblical worldview. He reminds us that humans—not tools—are moral agents. And that our use of AI must be guided not by novelty or efficiency, but by love of God and neighbor.

"Christians are called to resist being taken captive by empty philosophy," he writes, "and instead engage AI with wisdom, humility, and theological clarity."

His call is not for fear, but for formation. Not for withdrawal, but for discernment. In a world of accelerating tools, Thacker invites us to slow down and ask: What is this tool doing to me? And what kind of person is it helping me become?

This echoes a metaphor I shared earlier in the book: the axe. A simple tool. But one that forms the user. Learning to use an axe doesn't just shape your muscles—it reshapes your instincts. Over time, every tree begins to look like a target. The tool doesn't just serve you. It shapes you. AI is no different. It forms our habits, our posture, even our imagination. And so, Thacker's voice reminds us: discernment is not optional. It is discipleship.

Derek Schuurman—Virtue-by-Proxy vs. Virtue Amplification

Derek Schuurman, a Christian computer scientist and professor at Calvin University, offers one of the most thoughtful theological reflections on

---

8. Thacker, "Why Christians Should Care about Artificial Intelligence," para. 5.

AI I've encountered.⁹ In his article "Virtue and Artificial Intelligence," he makes a crucial distinction: AI can simulate virtue, but it cannot possess it. It can mimic empathy, but it cannot feel. It can nudge users toward good habits, but it cannot form character.

Schuurman introduces the idea of **"virtue-by-proxy"**—the notion that virtuous programmers can encode systems to reflect values like humility, civility, or justice. But he is clear-eyed about the limits. Christian formation, he argues, is not merely behavioral. It is relational. Communal. Spirit-empowered.

His alternative is **"virtue amplification"**—designing systems that support, rather than replace, the slow work of becoming Christlike. This is not about building artificial virtue. It's about building environments that make real virtue more likely.

This distinction—between simulation and formation—has deeply shaped my own thinking. In fact, Schuurman's influence runs deeper than this article. He is also a co-author of the *Christian Engineering Field Guide*, a book that has been formative for me personally and professionally.[10] That guide doesn't just offer technical advice—it offers a theological anthropology. It reminds us that engineers are not just problem-solvers. They are image-bearers. And their work is not just about efficiency—it's about love, justice, and stewardship.

I've referenced the *Field Guide* elsewhere in this book, but it's worth naming here again: it helped me see that engineering education must be about more than skills. It must be about virtue. And in the age of AI, that call is more urgent than ever.

Schuurman's voice reminds us that Christian formation cannot be outsourced. It must be embodied. And while AI may assist us, it cannot transform us. That work belongs to the Spirit—and to the slow, sacred rhythms of community, worship, and discipleship.

Tim Keller—The Alternate Intellectual Economy

Tim Keller didn't write extensively about artificial intelligence. But he didn't need to. His theological vision—clear, courageous, and deeply human—offers exactly the kind of grounding we need in this moment.

9. Schuurman, "Virtue."
10. Brue et al., *Field Guide*.

In his later writings, Keller spoke often about the need for an "alternate intellectual economy"—a way of thinking and living that resists the dominant cultural narratives of speed, self, and success. He believed that Christian institutions must offer more than critique. They must offer a counterculture. A place where wisdom is prized over novelty. Where care for people matters more than performance. Where the goal is not just to think differently, but to become different.

That vision has shaped this book more than I can say.

Keller's fingerprints are all over my story. *The Reason for God* was the book that found me—mis-shelved in a sci-fi section, at a moment when my life was unraveling.[11] His writing didn't argue to win. It reasoned to invite. It was clear, but never cold. Convicting, but never condemning. It opened the door to faith for me—and I walked through.

Later, *The Prodigal God* reframed everything I thought I knew about grace.[12] *Every Good Endeavor* helped me see engineering as a calling.[13] *The Meaning of Marriage* gave me language for both pain and hope.[14] And his essay on the decline and renewal of the church gave me a mission: to be part of that renewal.[15] To help build the alternate intellectual economy he envisioned.

This section of the chapter is not a citation. It's a thank-you. It's a tribute. It's a hinge.

Because Keller's vision is what this whole chapter—and maybe this whole book—is trying to live out. A vision of education that is not just reactive, but redemptive. Not just informed, but formed. Not just about what we know, but about who we are becoming.

In the age of AI, we don't just need better tools. We need better loves. And better liturgies. We need spaces where students can be formed not just as thinkers or workers, but as worshipers. That's the alternate economy. That's the call. And that's the legacy Keller leaves us.

You know the game where someone asks you who you'd have dinner with, anywhere in the world, if you could? When I encountered the writings of Tim Keller, I finally had my answer to that question. I never got to sit down with him. But I did get to hear him speak. I may have even met

11. Keller, *The Reason for God*.
12. Keller, *The Prodigal God*.
13. Keller, *Every Good Endeavor*.
14. Keller, *The Meaning of Marriage*.
15. Keller, "The Decline and Renewal of the American Church."

him briefly. Now, he's gone too soon. Even in his final days his grace in his sufferings was still an inspiration. I'd have loved to 'sit at his feet' and learn. To ask questions. To say thank you. His voice still echoes. And I hope this book is one of those in its small way.

Oxford Centre for Digital Theology / Papakostas—AI in Theological Education

The Oxford Centre for Digital Theology, along with scholars like Papakostas, has begun exploring how AI is reshaping theological education itself.[16] Their work is less about warning and more about wondering: What does it mean to teach theology in an age of algorithms? What does spiritual formation look like when students are shaped as much by screens as by Scripture?

These are not just theoretical questions. They're ones we're wrestling with on my own campus, too. That's why I've tried to draw closer to colleagues like **Jonathan Lett**, **Kelly Liebengood**, and **Luke Tallon**—each of whom has helped shape this book in ways both direct and profound.

Jonathan was my co-author on the original paper that introduced the t-shaped engineer model—an idea that has become the backbone of this book. His theological insight helped me see that formation isn't just about skills or relationships—it's about telos. About becoming.

Kelly was the first person I sent the original conference abstract to—the one that eventually became this book. I trusted his wisdom. And he didn't disappoint. He immediately named what had been nagging at me: that the theological core was underdeveloped. That the God at the center of it all needed to be clearer, stronger, more present. His feedback helped refine the heart of this project.

And Luke is working with me now on a project that asks a deceptively simple question: How deep is the faith development of our students? It's a question that cuts to the core of what Christian education is for. And it's one we're trying to answer not just with data, but with discernment.

The Oxford Centre's reflections echo these same concerns. They ask whether AI can assist in biblical language learning, sermon preparation, or spiritual direction. But they also ask deeper questions: Can a chatbot disciple? Can growth and development be automated? What happens when theological imagination is outsourced to a machine?

---

16. Papakostas, "Artificial Intelligence in Religious Education," 563.

Their answer, ultimately, is no. But their posture is not defensive. It's discerning. They call for institutions to engage AI not just as a tool, but as a test—a test of our theology, our pedagogy, and our trust in the Spirit's work.

Chapter 8 has gathered the voices shaping our moment—educators, theologians, engineers, and cultural critics—each offering insight into how AI is reshaping learning, identity, and formation. These voices—secular and sacred—remind us that AI is not just a technical tool. It is a cultural force. A spiritual test. A mirror held up to our pedagogy, our priorities, and our posture toward learning. In the next chapter, we turn from reflection to relationship—from what AI is doing to what we must do, together.

CHAPTER 9

Relational Breadth in a Disconnected Age

MY PERSONAL BOARD OF DIRECTORS

Some confessions here. First, I'm 52 years old. That feels quite old—until I say this next part: I still feel like I need mentorship.

At 52, I feel like I might have some wisdom. Something to say. A thought or two that might be worth listening to. And yet, I still need deep, anchoring relationships.

I didn't fully realize this need until I was nearing 40. I knew my dad had been influential (more on him in a moment), but I hadn't really appreciated it. I hadn't named it. Then, over lunch with an older colleague, I was introduced to the concept of a "personal board of directors." He said we all need people in our professional lives who listen, who care deeply about where we're going, and who have the wisdom, gravitas, and courage to speak into our lives—especially when we're headed in the wrong direction.

I've been lucky. I've had three. Now two. Let me explain.

My Dad

He's my stepdad, technically—but unless we're very close, you'll always hear me refer to him simply as my dad. We met when I was a teenager. He's been wonderful for our family: patient, kind, steady.

He's a professor at a Big State U. Almost to the end now. And fitting the theme of this book, he's retiring this fall. One of the prime reasons? Academia isn't what it used to be. Less concern for student well-being. More concern for research output and the bottom line.

His father was a professor at another Big State U. And his father before him—also a professor. Also Big State U. My dad is an engineer, and for years that meant I didn't want to be one. But as I matured, I realized engineering was for me. (By the way, my choice of discipline was purely relational—and I'll share that story later in this chapter.)

Now, we talk about engineering education all the time. He's been an award-winning Quarter Scale Tractor faculty advisor (which, in case you've missed all the concrete canoe stories scattered throughout this book, is *not* as cool as that!). We've swapped advisor advice back and forth for years, trying to help students grow.

Ron Welch

The second is Ron Welch—mentioned earlier in this book. He's a leader's leader. Vision in spades. Drive to match.

When he offered me my first academic position, it came with a caveat: "I want you to go to the ASCE training for faculty advisors your first fall." I said, "OK, sounds good." Then he added, "It starts before your contract does—early August. You'll need to get to Washington, D.C. to see it all. Your contract doesn't start until late August. Is that a problem?"

And then, with a smile: "Oh, by the way, our ASCE student chapter won't just be good—it will be great. I'm counting on you."

(Through the next half-dozen years, we were awarded Best Student Chapter in our region and were national finalists multiple times. No pressure indeed.)

Gulp. I guess not.

Joe Boylan

The third was Joe Boylan. I hired him to work for me at a previous institution. He had been Chief Engineer for a major company (you've heard of it). CEO of a major Christian organization. Retired Colonel out of West Point.

PART III. RELATIONAL AND THEOLOGICAL RESPONSE

In many ways, he was a second Ron Welch for me. Older. Craggier. Pricklier. He didn't understand academia as well—but he was unafraid to push. Hard.

He once told me that if someone said "No," he didn't hear "No." He heard, "Find another way." That could be exasperating. Sometimes you couldn't make him stop if the objective mattered to him. But he was wise. I believe that wisdom came from God. I'm sure of it. And, I also believe working for me was simply his 'finding another way' to mentor and pour into people—in this case the students and faculty all around him.

He passed away last week, as I was writing this book.

I had just sent him the article that became the seed for this manuscript. It was the last message I sent him. I thought he had more time. Turns out, he didn't.

His daughter sent me a message with a photo of a page from one of his many Bibles. With her permission, I share it here.

Photo of Joe's Bible

I can't count the number of colors and pens used to mark up those two pages. What a perfect example of deep, iterative, contextual thinking. What a deep life. A man of deep faith. So very important to my own formation.

These are the kinds of relationships I'm talking about in this chapter.

ANCHOR TO t-SHAPED (VERSUS T-SHAPED ENGINEERING HISTORY)

National Academy of Science authors note that "More than a quarter of a century ago, technology-intensive industries began calling for well-rounded or "T-shaped" workers, that is, those who combine deep knowledge and skills in a particular subject with broad, interdisciplinary, collaborative skills," and go on to reference efforts such as the ABET Engineering Criteria 2000, The NAE Engineer of 2020 efforts, and the efforts of many other stakeholders (e.g. ASCE, ASME, and NSPE) as attempts to address this issue.[1]

Thus, for 30 plus years in the secular space, there has been an identified need in the technology sector for workers with more than simply technical skills. In the early 1990's, Colin Palmer began to discuss hybrid-managers (a term coined by Michael Earl at Templeton College, Oxford)— those with an understanding of business and also the technical competence to understand the technical scope of information technology projects.[2,3] The term T-shaped was coined and used by David Guest in 1991 in *The Independent*—"these are a variation on Renaissance Man, equally comfortable with information systems, modern management techniques and the 12-tone scale."[4] Leonard-Barton in 1995 provided a pictorial representation of T-shaped skills, also identifying A-shaped and multi-lingual managers.[5] As originally coined, the term "T-shaped" referred to people with deep learning and skills in one technical area who could also function across multi-disciplinary teams (contrast with I-shaped). Medhat and Peers and Tranquillo discussed "those with technical depth as well as cross-disciplinary breadth."[6] However, in later years, T-shaped has come to mean combining "professional" skills with technical skills, with perhaps one of the earliest examples of this more 'modern' meaning in the literature from Dean James Plummer of Stanford in 2011, who discussed Stanford engineering turning out "capital Ts—vertically supported by strong math

1. Miller, "Why the Hard Science of Engineering. . ."; ABET, *Criteria for Accrediting Engineering Programs*. 1998; NAE, *Engineer of 2020*; ASCE, *Civil Engineering Body of Knowledge*; ASME, *Vision 2030*; NSPE, *Professional Engineering Body of Knowledge*.
2. Palmer, "'Hybrids'—A Critical Force."
3. Earl, *Management Strategies for Information Technology*.
4. Guest, "The Hunt Is On."
5. Leonard-Barton, *Wellsprings of Knowledge*.
6. Medhat and Peers, *T-Shaped Learning*; Tranquillo, "The T-Shaped Engineer."

PART III. RELATIONAL AND THEOLOGICAL RESPONSE

and science training but stretching laterally with extensive business and communication skills.[7]

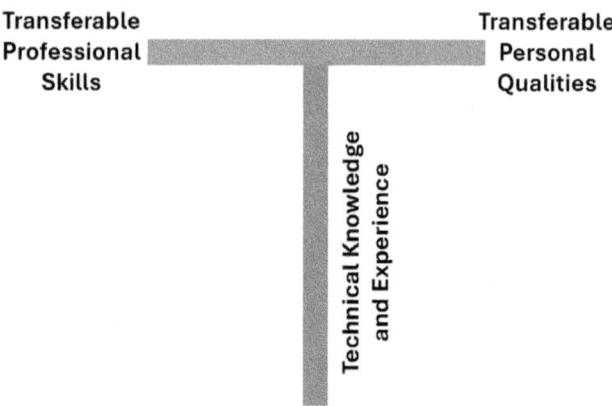

Historical Concept of the T-Shaped Engineer Influenced by Tranquillo

This vision found its way into accreditation standards. ABET, the body that accredits engineering programs in the U.S., embedded these relational and professional skills into its student outcomes.[8] The message was clear: engineering education must form more than just problem-solvers. It must form people who can work well with others.

Technical	Relational
ABET 1: Apply math, science, and engineering	ABET 3: Communicate
ABET 2: Perform Design	ABET 4: Ethical and professional skills
ABET 6: Experiments	ABET 5: Function on teams
ABET 7: Life-long learning	

ABET Outcomes

And yet, something was still missing.

The T-shaped model was a step forward—but not far enough. It assumed that the horizontal bar of relational skills was sufficient to guide the vertical bar of technical expertise. But what if both were floating? What if neither was grounded in something deeper?

7. Plummer, "Educating the Engineer of 2020."
8. ABET, *Criteria for Accrediting Engineering Programs*. 2025

That's where the t-shaped engineer comes in.

The vertical bar still represents technical depth. The horizontal bar still represents relational breadth. But the upward extension—the shape of the cross—represents something more: theological grounding. A vocational pursuit rooted in the love of God and neighbor.

This model doesn't just ask, "Can you work well with others?" It asks, "Do you love your neighbor?" It doesn't just ask, "Can you solve the problem?" It asks, "Is this problem worth solving?" It doesn't just ask, "Are you employable?" It asks, "Are you becoming the kind of person who reflects the character of Christ in your work?"

Jesus said the greatest commandment is to love God with all your heart, soul, mind, and strength—and the second is like it: to love your neighbor as yourself. The t-shaped engineer is an attempt to live that out in the world of engineering education.

As noted, the t-shaped engineering model goes further, refining these initial calls to more closely align with the second of Jesus' grand commandments to "love your neighbor as yourself."

FACULTY STUDY ON RELATIONSHIP SKILLS AND ITS IMPLICATIONS

In a recent survey, faculty members steeped in the t-shaped engineering model were asked to evaluate the importance of various 'soft' skills in the engineering curriculum. Each skill was rated on a five-point scale, and none received a score below 4.18. This reflects a strong consensus: relational and professional skills are not optional—they are essential. To better understand these results, we've grouped the ten skills into four thematic clusters.

Character and Formation

- Character and Ethics (4.81)
- Reliability, Time Management, and Work Ethic (4.51)

These skills reflect the internal compass of the engineer—the habits, virtues, and moral commitments that shape how one shows up in the world. That 'Character and Ethics' received the highest score is no surprise. In a t-shaped model, we are not merely educating; we are forming. These are not just professional traits—they are spiritual ones. They speak to who the student is becoming.

And here is the crux of the matter—**AI can't form character.** It can simulate ethical reasoning, but it can't cultivate virtue. The risk is that students may use AI to bypass the slow, formative work of perseverance, time management, or ethical wrestling. **The Opportunity** however is that Faculty can use AI as a mirror—asking students to compare their own reasoning with AI's and reflect on what's missing. In a world where AI can generate a code of ethics but not live by one, we must double down on forming students who can.

Communication and Expression

- Writing (4.73)
- Effective Business/Technical/Industry Presentations (4.69)

Engineers must be able to communicate clearly, persuasively, and with empathy. Whether through a written report or a spoken presentation, these skills are about making ideas accessible and actionable. In the age of AI—where machines can generate text and slides—human communication becomes even more critical. It's not just about what is said, but *how* and *why* it is said. These skills help students find their voice. As I discuss this bucket of skills with prospective students and their parents, I often bring up a lesson that I simply call "Email, Text or Phone Call." We discuss the virtues, pitfalls and challenges of each of these communication channels. This lesson is powerful, and the audience immediately grasps the importance of what I am trying to convey. They break into smiles and nods when I end with the phrase, "and sometimes, we must, gulp, actually go and talk with someone in person." We all recognize the power of the face-to-face. The power of presence.

Here, it is clear—**AI can write—but it can't connect.** It can generate grammatically correct prose, but it can't read the room, sense tone, or speak with conviction. We run the risk that students may outsource their voice to AI, losing the opportunity to develop clarity, empathy, and persuasion. They may not even know their own voice if AI has written everything for them in the past. Again, if engineering education is framed as a "Get-To" experience, then students NEED to 'Get-To,' so that their growth involves developing depth in this area. **Opportunity:** Use AI to draft, then revise with human nuance. Teach students to ask: *Does this sound like me? Does it serve others?* AI can help students find words, but only wholistic formation will help them find their voice.

Collaboration and Relational Intelligence

- Conflict Resolution (4.69)
- Teams and Teamwork (4.46)
- Human Connection (4.28)
- Client Relations (4.23)

This cluster represents the heart of relational breadth. These are the skills that allow engineers to work well with others—to navigate conflict, build trust, and lead with humility. In a world increasingly mediated by technology, these human capacities are more important than ever. AI can simulate conversation, but it cannot build relationships. It cannot resolve conflict with grace or lead with wisdom. These are sacred skills—essential for loving our neighbor well.

AI can simulate dialogue—but not relationship. It can role-play a teammate, but it can't build trust, resolve tension, or lead with humility. We risk students avoiding difficult conversations by letting AI mediate or replace them. The **Opportunity** may be to use AI to rehearse scenarios—but always return to real, embodied practice. "In the age of AI, the most human thing we can teach is may be how to be with others."

Professional Navigation

- Workplace Navigation (4.55)
- Supervision and Hierarchy (4.18)

This skill stands alone but is no less important. It reflects the ability to read context, understand organizational culture, and move wisely within systems. It's the meta-skill of professional maturity. In the t-shaped model, this is where relational breadth meets vocational discernment. AI may help us analyze systems, but it cannot teach us how to move through them with wisdom and integrity.

Together, these clusters paint a picture of the kind of engineer we hope to form: technically excellent, relationally wise, and theologically grounded. These are not just skills for the workplace—they are practices of love, humility, and care. And in the age of AI, they are more vital than ever. For a broader perspective on how AI is reshaping the value of human-centered skills in professional contexts, see Marinkovic in 2023.[9]

AI can map systems—but not navigate them wisely. It can analyze data, but it can't read a room, sense timing, or discern when to speak and when to listen. The risk in this space is students may mistake information for wisdom. **Opportunity**: Teach students to use AI as a tool for insight—but to rely on Biblical principles for discernment. AI can help you see the map. But only our Christian framework can help you walk the path.

THE FREE PROJECT AND THE FUTURE OF FORMATION

As I've wrestled with what it means to form t-shaped engineers in the age of AI, I've been encouraged to find others asking similar questions. One of the most promising efforts I've encountered is the Future-Ready Engineering Ecosystem (FREE) project, led by ASEE and funded by the National Science Foundation.[10]

I've had the privilege of serving on the national advisory board for this initiative. The FREE project brings together educators, industry leaders, and researchers to define the competencies engineers will need in a rapidly changing world—and to chart a path for how institutions can cultivate them.

What's striking is how closely the FREE framework aligns with the t-shaped model. The FREE Competency Taxonomy includes not only technical knowledge and skills, but also personal and professional attributes: integrity, empathy, collaboration, cultural awareness, and a commitment to the common good. These are not just workplace skills. They are distinctly relational. In fact, they are spiritual postures.

The FREE Rubric for Action goes further, offering a roadmap for change at every level—from individual faculty to entire institutions. It calls for modular, interdisciplinary, and competency-based learning.

9. Marinkovic, "The Shifting Importance of Soft Skills."
10. El-Sayed, DeLeeuw, and Korte, *Preparing Engineering Students for the Future.*

It challenges us to rethink how we assess success—not just by grades or GPAs, but by portfolios, projects, and the kind of people our students are becoming.

In short, the FREE project is a secular initiative with sacred resonance. It affirms what Christian educators have long believed: that education is not just about what students know, but about who they are becoming. And in the age of AI, that question—who are we becoming?—has never been more urgent.

THE IMPLICATIONS
INITIATIVE 2: HOST A FACULTY LUNCH-AND-LEARN ON PERMA

Faculty are not just transmitters of content—they are cultivators of culture. The way they teach, advise, and interact with students shapes not only what students learn, but how they experience learning. In a time when both students and educators are navigating fatigue, uncertainty, and rapid technological change, faculty well-being and motivation are essential to institutional flourishing.

This initiative draws on the **PERMA model** of well-being developed by psychologist Martin Seligman, which identifies five core elements of human flourishing: **Positive Emotion, Engagement, Relationships, Meaning, and Accomplishment.**[11]

Positive Emotion

Positive emotion is more than just feeling happy—it includes hope, gratitude, inspiration, and joy. In the classroom, cultivating positive emotion means creating moments that spark curiosity, celebrate small wins, and remind students (and faculty) why the work matters. It's not about avoiding difficulty, but about framing challenges in a way that invites engagement rather than dread. For Christian educators, this also includes joy rooted in grace—the deep assurance that our worth is not in our performance, but in being loved by God.

---

11. Seligman, *Flourish*.

PART III. RELATIONAL AND THEOLOGICAL RESPONSE

Engagement

Engagement is the experience of being fully absorbed in a task—what psychologists call "flow." It happens when students are challenged just enough to stretch, but not so much that they shut down. For faculty, it's the joy of teaching a class that clicks, or mentoring a student who's growing. In a PERMA-informed classroom, engagement is cultivated through active learning, real-world problems, and opportunities for students to use their strengths. It's about designing experiences that invite presence, not just compliance.

Relationships

Relationships are the glue of growth and development. They are the most consistent predictor of student thriving—and faculty thriving too. In the PERMA model, relationships refer to the sense of connection, trust, and belonging that comes from being known and cared for. For Christian educators, this is deeply theological: we are made in the image of a relational God. Classrooms that prioritize relationships—through mentoring, collaboration, and presence—become spaces where students are not just taught, but formed.

Meaning

Meaning is about purpose. It's the sense that what we're doing matters—and that it connects to something larger than ourselves. In education, meaning emerges when students see how their work contributes to human flourishing, when they connect their studies to their calling, and when they are invited to wrestle with the "why" behind the "what." For Christian institutions, this is a core strength: we can name the telos. We can say, with clarity and conviction, that our work is part of God's redemptive story.

Accomplishment

Accomplishment is not just about grades or awards—it's about growth. It's the sense of progress, mastery, and resilience that comes from setting goals and working toward them. In a PERMA-informed classroom, accomplishment is celebrated not only in outcomes, but in effort. Students are affirmed for perseverance, iteration, and courage. Faculty, too, need to feel that their work is making a difference—that they are helping students grow, and that their labor is not in vain.

These elements are not only psychologically beneficial—they are pedagogically powerful. When faculty experience purpose and connection in their work, they are more likely to foster those same qualities in their students.

But this initiative is not only about faculty flourishing—it's also about **equipping faculty to create environments where students can flourish**. The PERMA model offers a practical framework for designing classrooms that are not only intellectually rigorous but also emotionally and spiritually supportive. In this way, faculty become agents of growth, shaping spaces where students feel seen, challenged, and inspired.

Goal: Promote well-being and intrinsic motivation among faculty—and equip them to foster the same in their students.

Rationale: Faculty who are flourishing are more likely to create learning environments that are relational, resilient, and reflective. The PERMA model offers a research-based framework for understanding what makes teaching joyful and sustainable. It also resonates with a Christian vision of vocation: that our work is not just productive, but redemptive. When applied to classroom culture, PERMA helps students experience learning as meaningful, connected, and growth-oriented.

Action Steps:

- Organize a lunch-and-learn session introducing the PERMA model, with examples drawn from teaching, mentoring, and curriculum design. Note that lunch-and-learn fits our culture at *my* University. Another institution might pick a faculty workshop, a learning community, an on-line training module, an initiative by a teaching excellence center, or another format that fits *their* culture.
- Invite faculty to reflect on which PERMA elements are most present—and most absent—in their current teaching experience.
- Provide practical strategies for integrating PERMA into classroom culture:

- **Positive Emotion**: Begin class with a moment of gratitude or curiosity.
- **Engagement**: Use active learning techniques that invite participation and flow.
- **Relationships**: Build rapport through office hours, feedback, and shared projects.
- **Meaning**: Connect course content to real-world impact and Christian vocation.
- **Accomplishment**: Celebrate progress, not just performance.

- Include a segment on how PERMA can be used to **design assignments, feedback, and classroom rituals** that support student flourishing.
- Follow up with a short survey to assess changes in faculty mindset and morale, as well as perceived impact on student engagement.

THE SCIENCE AND SPIRIT OF FLOURISHING

When we first proposed a faculty lunch-and-learn on PERMA, it felt like a small step—an experiment in well-being. But the more I've studied the research, the more convinced I've become: this isn't just a nice-to-have. It's a formational imperative.

A recent study by McCave and Maczka piloted a two-course sequence for non-calculus-ready engineering students.[12] Alongside physics and computational modeling, students engaged in weekly well-being sessions grounded in the PERMA model. The results were mixed—but revealing. Engagement rose. Confidence grew. Students valued the well-being content. But they also wanted more: more integration, more reinforcement, more presence.

The lesson? Well-being can't be an add-on. It must be embedded. It must be lived.

That's why this initiative matters. Faculty are not just transmitters of content—they are thermostats of culture. When they understand the science of flourishing, they can design classrooms that are not only rigorous, but redemptive.

12. Maczka and McCave, "Integrating Computation."

And the science is compelling. Kern expands PERMA into PERMAH—adding Health as a sixth pillar—and offers practical strategies for embedding it into school culture.[13] Kovich et al. validate PERMA's structure with over 5,000 undergraduates, finding that all five elements predict well-being.[14] And Kern & Benecchi go further still, exploring how PERMA aligns with Christian theology—especially in its emphasis on gratitude, hope, and virtue.[15]

But they also name the tension: positive psychology often centers the self. Christianity centers God. That's where theological grounding matters. That's where the t-shaped engineer comes in.

This initiative isn't just about boosting morale. It's about forming people. It's about helping faculty see their work not just as instruction—but as invitation. Not just as performance—but as presence.

Because in the age of AI, the most human thing we can do is care.

INITIATIVE 3: OFFER A STUDENT WORKSHOP ON AI PROMPTING AND BEST PRACTICES

For many students, AI tools have become a default companion—used late at night, under pressure, and often without guidance. While these tools can support learning, they can also short-circuit it. When students rely on AI to complete tasks without understanding the underlying concepts, they risk becoming passive consumers rather than active thinkers.

This initiative addresses the need for AI literacy that is both technical and ethical. It draws on research in metacognition and self-regulated learning, which shows that students benefit from explicit instruction in how to use tools reflectively and strategically.[16] It also aligns with Christian formation: discernment is not just about what we can do, but what we ought to do.

Goal: Equip students to use AI as a tool for learning, not shortcutting.

Rationale: Students who understand how AI works—and how to work with it—are better prepared for the future of engineering. They are also more likely to retain agency in their learning process. Teaching students

---

13. Kern, "PERMAH: A Useful Model."
14. Kovich et al., "Application of the PERMA Model."
15. Kern and Benecchi, *Intersections of Positive Psychology and Christianity*.
16. Zimmerman, "Becoming a Self-Regulated Learner."

PART III. RELATIONAL AND THEOLOGICAL RESPONSE

how to prompt, evaluate, and iterate with AI fosters intellectual humility, curiosity, and responsibility.

Action Steps:

- Host a hands-on workshop open to all students, ideally early in the semester. While we use the term student workshop here, this initiative can be reframed to fit the culture and rhythms of different institutions. At a research university, it might take the form of a co-curricular seminar series or a "digital fluency" badge program. At a liberal arts college, it could be embedded in a first-year experience course or offered as a faculty-student roundtable. At a community college, it might be a one-credit micro-course or a hands-on lab session during orientation. The format is flexible—the goal is creating an environment where positive growth and change can happen.
- Topics covered:
  - How generative AI models work (brief overview).
  - How to write effective prompts for different tasks (e.g., coding, summarizing, brainstorming).
  - How to evaluate AI responses for accuracy, bias, and depth.
  - How to use AI for ideation, revision, and exploration—not just answers.
- Include discipline-specific examples (e.g., engineering design prompts, technical writing, data analysis).
- Provide a follow-up resource guide with sample prompts, ethical guidelines, and reflection questions.
- Encourage faculty to assign a short reflection after the workshop: "How might you use AI in your learning this semester? What boundaries will you set?"

This initiative supports both axes of the 2x2 matrix: it enhances students' ability to use AI well, while also helping them develop the discernment to know when not to. It reinforces the idea that AI is not a replacement for thinking—but a partner in the process of becoming a thoughtful, ethical engineer.

VOCATION, DISCERNMENT, AND THE DRAMA OF FORMATION

At my university, we talk often about vocation—quite distinct from the word career, or the concept of a job. Viewing our professional pursuits as a working out of our ultimate purpose, our calling. Training students to think not just about what they will do, but who they are becoming.

That's why this workshop matters.

In the age of AI, students are not just learning new tools. They are being shaped by them. And if we don't help them reflect on that shaping, we risk forming engineers who are technically fluent but ethically fragile.

Christian education must go deeper. It must ask: What kind of person is this tool forming me to be? What kind of world is it helping me build?

This is not just a question of academic integrity. It's a question of vocation. Of calling. Of character. And it's a question of ethics.

Because every use of AI is a moral act. It reflects a set of values—about truth, labor, authorship, and responsibility. When students use AI to bypass struggle, they're not just saving time. They're making a decision about what kind of learner—and what kind of person—they want to be.

Christian ethics calls us to more. It reminds us that we are not autonomous agents, but image-bearers. That our work is not just output, but offering. That our choices—even digital ones—are part of our witness.

And it's a question that must be asked within the larger story of Scripture—not as a list of disconnected rules, but as a coherent drama of creation, fall, redemption, and restoration. As *God and the Drama of Scripture* reminds us, we are not just readers of the Bible—we are participants in its story.[17] And that story calls us to live wisely, love sacrificially, and steward creation—including technology—with care.

This workshop is a small but vital step in that direction. It's not just about prompting better. It's about prompting deeper. It's about helping students see AI not as a shortcut, but as a site of discernment.

Because in the end, our students are not just preparing for careers. They are preparing for lives of faithful presence in a world of accelerating change.

And that formation begins with a simple question:

---

17. Bartholomew and Goheen, *Drama of Scripture*.

PART III. RELATIONAL AND THEOLOGICAL RESPONSE

How will I use this tool—and who will I become in the process?

CONCLUSION

Remember back when I told you I'd explain why I chose the engineering discipline that I did? Here's the skinny.

I was a bit adrift in college. A National Merit Scholar who was barely passing most of my classes. I just wasn't that interested. I had tried English, Psychology, History, even Math.

Eventually, I figured out the problem: I didn't feel challenged. So I made a decision—I signed up for engineering (remember how I said my Dad was an engineer—yes, it was time, and I finally was taking the plunge). I was going to be a Mechanical.

At the same time, a friend of mine down the hall—also switching from English to engineering—was making the leap. Yes, we'd both read a lot of Shakespeare. And yes, it does seem odd in retrospect that two English majors would pivot to engineering at the same time, when all roads seem to generally lead the opposite way. Providence? Couldn't be.

The only problem was that he wanted to be Civil. I was set on Mechanical. I tried to convince him. He wouldn't budge. Finally, I relented. I went Civil.

I have no regrets. But looking back, it's clear that the ultimate reason I chose Civil wasn't technical—it was relational. I didn't want to go in alone. I needed a partner. A teammate. This was the beginning of my first academic community.

And here I am today, writing about it.

Relational breadth is not a soft skill—it's a sacred one. In an age of disconnection and digital drift, engineers must be formed not only to collaborate, but to care. Chapter 9 has explored the power of mentorship, emotional intelligence, and community in shaping whole people. But relationships alone are not enough. They must be rooted in something deeper. Chapter 10 turns our attention to that foundation: God. If we are to achieve the second half of the Greatest commandment well, to love our neighbor, we must attend to the first part, to love the Lord our God. Chapter 10 will provide an explicit theological grounding to the entire t-shaped engineer approach.

CHAPTER 10

Theological Grounding in a Secular Age

Note, I've structured this Chapter around the beginning (Genesis), three of the most personal and personally shattering portions of the Bible, and the end (the City of Revelation). While the beginning and end sections naturally bookend the five movements, the middle three are not in a particular order, jumping from a parable told by Jesus, back to a specific but often missed moment described in Genesis, and concluding with an examination of one of Paul's most famous letters. I've included raw reflections on these bookends and the three central movers—I am not a trained theologian, what I've provided is a lay point of view for a book about the digital age and our current moment, modeling the relational style that we need to train our engineers to grasp.

Garden
Genesis

Genesis
Question

Luke
Prodigal Parable

Romans
Call

City
Revelation

Theological Grounding

PART III. RELATIONAL AND THEOLOGICAL RESPONSE

IN THE BEGINNING

I'll begin this chapter in a way that you might expect—in the beginning. Quoting from my coauthor on an earlier paper that introduced the t-shaped engineer as a concept,

> "Genesis 1 affirms [an] intrinsic connection between the order of creation and its goodness and telos by using repetition and pattern to teach that God ordered the world to facilitate eternal communion with God. In the first three days of the cosmos, God creates space for creaturely life by making boundaries. God forms limits between light and dark, sea and sky, and then carves a border between the sea and dry land. Each limit God imposes brings order out of chaos. God then fills each space with life on days 4–6, with fish, birds, vegetation, animals, and finally human beings. The limits that structure the world exist to promote life and flourishing, not impede it. The purpose of these six days is revealed in the seventh: rest with God. Every aspect of creation exists to furnish intimacy between God and his creation.

The Genesis creation account also communicates something about the nature of this order: the text's exquisite and delicate form of order, pattern, and rationality requires patience, attention, and an appreciation for poetry (the primary mode for biblical speech about creation). This means that engineers must not imagine the order of creation to be modelled on the machine and as purely a technical realm. Genesis puts forward different metaphors: a poem and the religious architecture of a temple. The ordering of the world is replete with profound transcendent meaning, and Christian engineers seek to work within this order by apprehending the way that the natural order reflects this goal. The Christian proclamation that creation is good and intelligible is the basis for both the scientific study of the world (i.e. the technical aspect of the t-shaped model) and the social and political organization of human communities (i.e. the relational aspect of the t-shaped model) according to the created order."[1]

Since I am not the theologian that my coauthor on that paper, Dr. Jonathan Lett is, I'll simply note an observation first pointed out to me by Brue, Shuurman, and Vanderleest in the *Christian Engineering Field Guide*.[2]

Each day God creates—giving magnitude and direction (purpose)

---

1. McGinnis and Lett "Engineering, Meaning and Faith."
2. Brue, Schuurman, and VanderLeest, *A Christian Field Guide to Technology*.

- Stars to separate day from night, birds to fly, fish to swim, trees to fruit, etc.
- Each day God saw that it was Good.

Then God created mankind as image bearers and put all of creation in relationship with one another: "Fill the earth and subdue it. Rule over the fish in the sea . . . I give you every seed-bearing plant . . . I give every green plant for food" (Gen 1:28–30 NIV).

All of creation in relationship, with magnitude and direction (pointing toward God)—only then was it very good—while the world is good as each piece is created, it is only "very good" when ordered and arranged in relationship, a key piece of the t-shaped engineering model, and a key piece of how AI and the current digital world are distorting what it means to be and flourish as a human.

A second note here concerns work. It is a misconception to believe that work was a consequence of the fall—there was work in the Garden prior to the fall,. This leads us to the conclusion that engineering can be seen as a holy calling—a sacred vocation.

Whether one reads Genesis as literal history or sacred metaphor, its theological vision remains clear: we are made for relationship, for meaningful work, and for communion with God.

If Genesis gives us a vision of creation ordered in relationship and purpose, then the question becomes: what happens when that order is broken? When we forget who we are, or what we're for? In a world shaped by performance, distraction, and digital metrics, we don't just lose our way—we lose our identity.

That's where grace begins. And that's where we turn next: to a story not just about rebellion, but about return. A story that reminds us who we are, and whose we are.

"THE FATHER WHO RUNS" → OUR IDENTITY IN GOD

Before diving into the reflection, let's briefly revisit the parable Jesus tells in Luke 15:11–32, often called *The Parable of the Prodigal Son*. It's one of the most beloved and theologically rich stories in Scripture, and it serves as a powerful anchor for the kind of theological grounding this chapter explores.

PART III. RELATIONAL AND THEOLOGICAL RESPONSE

The Story in Five Movements

1. **The Younger Son's Rebellion**

   * A younger son demands his inheritance early—a shocking request that dishonors his father.
   * He leaves home and squanders everything in reckless living.

2. **The Crisis and Return**

   * Destitute and humiliated, he takes a job feeding pigs.
   * In desperation, he decides to return home and confess his sin, hoping to be treated as a hired servant.

3. **The Father's Radical Response**

   * While the son is still far off, the father sees him, runs to him, and embraces him.
   * He restores the son fully—robe, ring, sandals—and throws a celebratory feast.

4. **The Older Son's Resentment**

   * The older son, who stayed and worked faithfully, is angry at the celebration.
   * He refuses to join the feast, feeling overlooked and bitter.

5. **The Father's Invitation**

   * The father pleads with the older son, affirming his place and inviting him into joy.
   * The parable ends unresolved—leaving the reader to consider their own response.

The Prodigal Son for me, in humbleness, should probably be better known as 'The Man with Two Sons.' Sometimes I am the younger—lost and wandering far from home. Sometimes the older, judging in my pride, just as lost. Which is it? Thankfully the third character in the story is truly the prodigal—prolifically, recklessly extravagant in the ways he heaps gifts, favor and grace on his sons. The father who MUST have been waiting on the porch looking out, searching always for his lost son to return. The father who begs his older son to come into the feast. Who knows how lost that son is and loves, loves, loves anyway. The father who, "while he (the younger son) was still a long way off, saw him and was filled with compassion for him; he ran to his son, threw his arms around him and kissed him." (NIV) This is the Prodigal God who runs for me. And I am so very grateful. (This reflection is based on my gleanings from Tim Keller's wonderful book—Prodigal God.)[3]

I will also add here that this book was inspired by another quote from Keller describing conditions necessary for a renewal of the American church:[4]

> "There is a robust, respected, and growing community of intellectuals and scholars that hold unashamedly to historic Christian doctrine who are (a) active in every academic field of inquiry, producing scholarship that contributes to and alters the field, (b) a growing presence in universities, and (c) inaugurating an entire alternate intellectual economy of study centers, think tanks, academies, periodicals, and publishing."

I want to be part of this renewal. This book was specifically inspired by this call and seeks to become a step on the journey in providing timely, context sensitive scholarship in the area of engineering education.

This reflection speaks to **grace as the foundation of identity**. In a world where AI can measure, optimize, and evaluate, students need to know that their worth is not in their performance—but in being loved by a God who runs toward them.

t-Shaped Connection:

The upward bar of the "t" is about Christ-centered purpose. This story reminds us that our students are not just future professionals—they are beloved children of God. That's the starting point for any meaningful development of wisdom.

If the story of the Prodigal Son reminds us who we are—beloved children pursued by grace—then the story of Eden reminds us how God relates to us even when we hide.

---

3. Keller, *Prodigal God*.
4. Keller, "The Decline and Renewal of the American Church."

PART III. RELATIONAL AND THEOLOGICAL RESPONSE

Identity is foundational, but presence is formational. And in the quiet moment after the fall, we encounter a God who does not shout, but asks. A God who does not condemn first, but calls gently: "Where are you?"

This is the next movement in our theological grounding—not just being known, but being invited.

"THE GOD WHO ASKS" → THEOLOGICAL GROUNDING AS PRESENCE

Picture Adam and Eve in the Garden. Naked, having Fallen, and now afraid. Hiding from God. And what is His response? Does He reach down, grab them by their newly made shirt collars, and haul them up to be berated? Does He smite with lightning and thunder from afar? He does not. He is calm, full of Grace. Asks a simple question—"Where are you?" This is the God of the Universe. Omniscient. Omnipotent. Does He know where they are? Of course He does. Then why ask? Pure Grace. He allows Adam and Eve to explain themselves. He gives them the dignity of being able to give a response. Yes, there are consequences, but they are meted out with love. It didn't have to be this way. But it is. Thank God.

This reflection highlights **God's posture of invitation**. In contrast to AI's predictive certainty, God asks questions—not because He lacks knowledge, but because He honors relationship.

God's question—"Where are you?"—is not a request for information. It's an invitation to relationship. It's a moment of profound restraint and grace. The omniscient Creator of the universe already knows where Adam and Eve are. But He asks anyway.

This is a deeply theological moment—but it's also a profoundly pedagogical one. In a world increasingly shaped by AI, where answers are instant and efficiency is prized, we must remember that learning is not just about information transfer. It's about formation. And that requires space. It requires questions. It requires the dignity of the learner.

Too often, education becomes a performance—students jumping through hoops, producing outputs, optimizing for grades. But what if we took our cue from the garden? What if we saw our students not as problems to be solved, but as people to be invited? What if we asked more questions—not because we don't know the answers, but because we want them to grow?

This is the posture of the teacher who reflects the heart of God: not one who dominates the room with knowledge, but one who creates space for discovery. One who listens. One who waits. One who honors the learner's voice.

In the age of AI, this kind of teaching is more important than ever. Because while machines can deliver answers, only humans can offer presence. Only humans can ask the kind of questions that form souls.

t-Shaped Connection

This models the kind of relational breadth we want to cultivate. It also reminds us that Christ-centered purpose isn't just about doctrine—it's about how we show up: with curiosity, humility, and grace.

If God's question in the garden—"Where are you?"—invites us into presence, then Paul's cry in Rom 7 reveals what we often find when we arrive: a divided heart.

Even when we know what is good, we struggle to do it. Even when we long for wholeness, we feel the fracture. This is not a failure of knowledge—it's a condition of the soul.

And yet, the story doesn't end in despair. Because the God who asks also delivers.

AI IS THE TIP OF THE ICEBERG

We talk a lot about AI in this book—but it's really the surface. Beneath it lies the digital age: the smartphones, the social feeds, the dopamine loops, the curated selves. AI didn't create this world. But it's accelerating it. And if we want to form students who can thrive in it, we have to address the whole iceberg—not just the tip.

PART III. RELATIONAL AND THEOLOGICAL RESPONSE

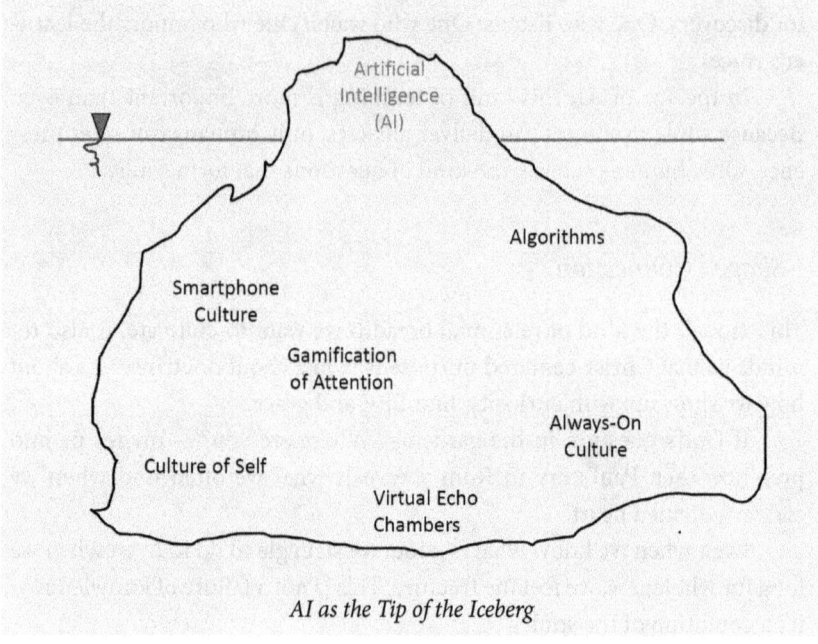

AI as the Tip of the Iceberg

"THE GOSPEL THAT DELIVERS" → GOD AS HOPE

From Rom 7:

> "15 I do not understand what I do. For what I want to do I do not do, but what I hate I do. 16 And if I do what I do not want to do, I agree that the law is good. 17 As it is, it is no longer I myself who do it, but it is sin living in me. 18 For I know that good itself does not dwell in me, that is, in my sinful nature. For I have the desire to do what is good, but I cannot carry it out. 19 For I do not do the good I want to do, but the evil I do not want to do—this I keep on doing. 20 Now if I do what I do not want to do, it is no longer I who do it, but it is sin living in me that does it." (NIV)

This is a powerful commentary on my own life—often we know what is right but cannot achieve it, either the whole or in part. I love how this portion of Paul's letter ends though—right back to the gospel again.

> "24 What a wretched man I am! Who will rescue me from this body that is subject to death? 25 Thanks be to God, who delivers me through Jesus Christ our Lord!" (NIV)

Romans 7 is a raw, honest look at the human condition. It names the inner conflict that AI cannot resolve. But it doesn't end in despair—it ends in deliverance. We have the hope of Jesus.

t-Shaped Connection:

This is the telos. The "why" behind the "what." The reason we form engineers who can persevere, love, and discern. Because we are not just forming minds—we are forming souls. And souls need hope.

If the gospel delivers us from despair and reorients us toward hope, then the question becomes: how do we live—and teach—in light of that hope?

Our identity in Christ is not just a comfort. It's a calling. It shapes how we think, how we teach, and how we prepare students to engage a world increasingly shaped by artificial intelligence.

So what does this mean for our classrooms, our curricula, and our students? Before we turn to the fifth initiative, let me share a story I often tell my students—a parable of sorts about formation, value, and the choices we make.

A MENTOR'S VOICE—WHAT DOES IT MEAN TO BE HUMAN?

Remember in Chapter 9 when I introduced my "Board of Directors"? It's time to hear from another who has gradually worked his way into a seat in that room—Dr. Paul Leiffer. Since I'll be quoting some of the works of the apostle Paul in this section, I'll refer to my friend Paul here as Paul L.

Paul L. is an emeritus professor at my university, where he served for over 40 years. He's warm, kind, and soft-spoken. When I once told him, "I haven't found my people yet at LeTourneau," and explained the concept of the Board of Directors, he didn't say much. Instead, he showed up. Every few weeks, a calendar invite appears in my inbox: "Lunch, Mike?" He comes prepared—with news clippings, thoughtful questions, and a notepad. He listens. He follows up. He mentors.

He also cares deeply about engineering education. So deeply, in fact, that he wrote his own book: *Engineering Through the Lens of Faith*.[5] One of its ap-

---

5. Leiffer, *Engineering Through the Lens of Faith*.

PART III. RELATIONAL AND THEOLOGICAL RESPONSE

pendices, titled *What Does It Mean to Be Human?*, offers a rich theological anthropology that complements and deepens the reflections in this chapter.

In that piece, Paul L. draws on Scripture and the work of philosopher Mortimer Adler to remind us that we are not gods, animals, or machines.[6] We are not "brains on a stick" or "computers made of meat." We are image-bearers—created by God, known by God, and made for relationship, creativity, and worship.

Adler's framework is especially helpful in our current moment. He identifies seven characteristics that distinguish humans from animals—traits that no AI, no matter how advanced, can replicate:

Discursive Language: Only humans use propositional language—sentences, symbols, and abstract thought. AI can mimic syntax, but it cannot mean.

Technological Creativity: Only humans invent tools, build shelters, and fabricate clothing. AI can optimize, but it cannot originate.

Moral and Political Agency: Only humans create laws and organize society. AI can enforce rules, but it cannot discern justice.

Historical Consciousness: Only humans transmit culture across generations. AI has no memory of meaning—only data.

Religious Capacity: Only humans engage in worship, ritual, and the search for transcendence. AI has no soul to lift.

Ethical Awareness: Only humans possess conscience—a sense of right and wrong. AI has no moral compass.

Aesthetic Expression: Only humans create art for beauty's sake. AI can generate images, but it cannot behold.

These traits are not evolutionary accidents. They are echoes of divine design. As Paul L. writes, we are "fearfully and wonderfully made" (Ps. 139:14), designed for dominion, community, and glory. In a world increasingly tempted to remake humanity through technology, Paul L's reminder is timely: what we try to create through AI or transhumanism, Christ has already made possible through grace. "If anyone is in Christ," Paul L. writes, "he is a new creation" (2 Cor. 5:17).

Paul L.'s vision reminds us that theological grounding isn't abstract—it's embodied, relational, and essential to how we understand ourselves in an

---

6. Adler, *The Difference of Man*

age of machines. As I explore my technical work and challenges, my work in building relationships at a new place, and the thing that really matters, pursuing God, I am grateful to have him in my life.

THE WORLD'S GREATEST BANANA SALESMAN

I have a story I tell at the beginning of the semester—usually to seniors. By that point, I've built up trust with them. They know I'm probably going somewhere with it, and they're willing to go along for the ride.

I begin simply: "I AM the World's Greatest Banana Salesman."

Skeptical looks? A raised eyebrow? At least one student who started class looking bored now sitting straight up with a "You've got to be kidding me—this is what we're talking about today?" expression? Yes, yes, and yes.

I double down. Yep, I'm the World's Greatest Banana Salesman, and I can prove it. I ask for a volunteer—someone willing to have some fun and not lose the thread. I offer them 12 bananas for $5. Will they buy them? Sometimes they say yes, sometimes no. Maybe it depends on whether the class is before or after lunch. I digress. Whatever the answer, here comes the fun part.

I say: I know I offered you 12 bananas for $5, but I have a MUCH better deal. I know you'll take it. I'm certain. In a spirit of generosity, here's my final offer: 6 bananas for $5. What a bargain, right? A steal. I know you want this. It's so much better, right?

I build it up. I make them see the absurdity I'm trying to put over on them in such an obvious, bald-faced way—to get them to accept that less for the same price is more. We all get to a point where we're a bit confused as to why I might try to do this to them. We see the perfect absurdity of it all.

Then I pivot.

This is EXACTLY what you're doing to your education here at our university if you're not careful. If a professor offers to cancel class, you celebrate. But wait—that's one less banana. If you cut corners on an assignment, copy from a friend, use AI when you needed to wrestle with something— one less banana. Skip class? Down another. Not get involved with a student organization? You must really not like the bananas we're offering.

You're paying the same amount in time and money—grab ALL the bananas you can. Be greedy for them. Hungry for them. Don't let the World's

Greatest Banana Salesman—or anyone else, including yourself—convince you to take a sucker's deal.

This story, I realized as I was preparing this book, is essentially the parable of the talents retold—what will we do with what we have been given? As educators, we have been given much and aim to deliver much. The fourth initiative describes how we might give students something deliberately more in the AI and formation space, with the hope that they tend the skills we develop, growing them for their own future.

INITIATIVE 4: PROPOSE A NEW GENERAL EDUCATION COURSE—"AI AND HUMAN FLOURISHING"

The rise of AI is not just a technical revolution—it is a philosophical and theological one. As machines increasingly perform tasks once thought to require human intelligence, we are forced to ask: What does it mean to be human? What is our work for? What is our worth when machines can outperform us in tasks we once considered uniquely ours?

This initiative proposes a new course within our University's general education core, specifically under the "Topics in Technology and Human Flourishing" category. This category is designed to foster interdisciplinary engagement with contemporary technological issues through a Christian lens. Courses in this area are expected to be team-taught, draw from multiple disciplines, and address the ethical, cultural, and theological dimensions of technology.

Goal: Create space for ethical, philosophical, and theological exploration of AI's role in society.

Rationale: Students need more than technical fluency—they need a moral center. A general education course on AI and human flourishing invites students to wrestle with the big questions: What kind of world are we building? What kind of people are we becoming? How can we use technology in ways that honor God and serve others?

This course would directly support several general education learning outcomes (note, I've listed my University's germane outcomes here—most deeply Christian institutions would have something similar in place):

- **SLO2**: Interpret the world in contemporary contexts
- **SLO4**: Deliver effective oral presentations
- **SLO6**: Demonstrate cultural competence within a theological framework

- **SLO7**: Articulate an informed Christian vision of human flourishing

It would also reinforce key ABET outcomes for engineering students:

- **ABET 3**: Communicate effectively with a range of audiences
- **ABET 4**: Recognize ethical and professional responsibilities in engineering contexts
- **ABET 5**: Function effectively on a team with leadership and collaboration

Action Steps:

- Develop and submit a course proposal to the General Education Curriculum Committee. Note that the approval process and governance structure at each institution may be different—the concept is the key.
- Suggested course title: "AI and Human Flourishing: Technology, Ethics, and the Christian Ethos."
- Core themes might include:
  - The history and future of AI: from Turing to transformers.
  - Human identity and creativity in the age of machines.
  - The anchoring framework of the t-shaped engineer.
  - Theological anthropology: what Scripture says about work, wisdom, and worth.
  - AI's impact on labor, relationships, justice, and meaning.
  - Practical AI literacy: how to use AI tools wisely and ethically.
- Course assignments could include:
  - A personal technology audit and reflection.
  - A case study analysis of an AI-related ethical dilemma.
  - A final project proposing a redemptive use of AI in a chosen field.
  - A team presentation on a contemporary AI issue, integrating technical, ethical, and theological perspectives.

This initiative supports the "AI-proofing" quadrant of the 2x2 matrix by helping students develop the inner resources to resist dehumanizing uses of technology. It also reinforces the "get-to" mindset by framing learning as a journey toward wisdom, not just utility. Most importantly, it invites students to see themselves not just as users of technology, but as stewards of it—called to shape the future with clarity, courage, and Christ-centered purpose.

FAITH FORMATION BY DESIGN— WHAT THE DATA REVEALS

For decades, Christian universities have hoped that students would grow in faith during their college years. Some have tried to measure this. A few have studied the pathways. But for STEM students—especially engineers—little data existed to show whether that growth was happening, or what was driving it.

That's beginning to change.

A 2025 survey of over 250 engineering students at LeTourneau University revealed statistically significant growth in faith across nearly every dimension—from prayer and Scripture engagement to vocational clarity and love of neighbor. Students who experienced the greatest growth ("High Changers") consistently rated their Bible and Theology courses as more impactful than their peers did. In fact, this was the only individual practice that showed a statistically significant difference between High and Low Changers.

The takeaway? Curriculum matters. And so does intentionality.

This aligns with a growing recognition across Christian higher education: while engineering faculty are well-equipped to teach technical content, they often lack evidence-based tools for supporting students' spiritual development. A recent grant proposal to the Louisville Institute identified this as a critical gap. Despite the centrality of faith formation in Christian mission statements, there is no widely adopted framework for how STEM faculty can meaningfully contribute to that formation—especially in disciplines where faith is often seen as peripheral.

This is where Initiative 4 comes in. A course on "AI and Human Flourishing" doesn't just fill a curricular gap—it creates a formational opportunity. AI is not a neutral topic. It raises urgent questions about identity, purpose, agency, and ethics. In other words, it invites theological reflection. By anchoring this course in both technical literacy and Christian anthropology, we give students a space to wrestle with what it means to be human in an age of machines—and what it means to follow Christ in a world increasingly shaped by algorithms.

Initiative 4 is not just about ethics. It's about growth. It's about creating space for students to ask the questions that matter most—about work, worship, and witness.

Because faith development doesn't happen by accident.

It happens by design.

THE ENDING: WORK IN THE CITY

We began this chapter in a garden—ordered, relational, and good. We end in a city—radiant, redeemed, and whole.

In Rev 21, we see the culmination of God's story: a city where God dwells with His people, where work is no longer toil, and where the glory of the nations is brought in. This is not a return to Eden—it is something greater. It is the fulfillment of every longing, the restoration of every fracture.

And in that city, there is work. There is design. There is beauty. There is purpose.

This is the telos of engineering—not just to build what is possible, but to participate in what is good. Not just to optimize, but to love. Not just to train minds, but to form souls.

In the age of AI, we must remember: we are not just preparing students for jobs. We are preparing them for eternity.

This has been my rationale for why God belongs at the center of engineering. He was there at the beginning, and He'll be there at the end—providing meaningful work that allows engineers to tend His creation at every stage. In between, He has revealed His character in all the ways that matter, showing us how we ought to live and lead. Any close reading of Scripture leads to a simple but profound conclusion: the standard definition of engineering—using math and science to solve problems—is woefully incomplete. Unless it is married to and infused with the Greatest Commandment—to love God and love people—engineering becomes a soulless enterprise. But with this radically complete definition, it becomes a t-shaped holy vocation. And that changes everything. The next chapter explores how faculty can shepherd the next generation into this calling—into lives of purpose, presence, and formation.

CHAPTER 11

From 'Have-To' to 'Get-To'— Faculty at the Center

A DEAR FRIEND

Let me tell you about my closest faculty colleague, Mike Gangone.

When Mike arrived at my former institution for his interview, you could tell he was nervous. As part of our culture, we always invited students to join the faculty for the first night's interview dinner. We believed strongly that students should have a voice in shaping the community—and little did I know how true that would turn out to be.

That night, the students told Mike that "all" of the professors at our school used a very specific color scheme when writing on the board: blue for titles, red for forces, black for basics, green for dimensions, and so on. (This came straight from the ExCEEd teaching model, which emphasizes structured learning through visual cues. At one point, we may have been the only civil engineering program in the country where every full-time faculty member had attended ExCEEd.)

Mike was scheduled to teach a sample class the next day. That night, back at the hotel, he rewrote all his notes—this time using a rainbow of colors that I'm not sure even Crayola had names for. The next morning, his lecture was. . . vivid. The students were a bit confused—there were colors

FROM 'HAVE-TO' TO 'GET-TO'—FACULTY AT THE CENTER

everywhere, but no discernible pattern. Still, the important thing wasn't the color scheme. It was that he listened. He responded. He cared.

Since then, Mike has gone on to win several of the most prestigious teaching awards in the country. He is, quite simply, an extraordinary teacher.

There's more. Mike is a structural engineer, just like me. At a small school, that raised a question: could we share the structures track? There weren't many classes. I'd seen others struggle to collaborate in similar situations. But from Day 1, we split the courses evenly—and became good friends in the process. (Mike is a very large man, and yet, because of his kindness, students affectionately called him the "little spoon" and me the "big spoon." We were always seen together.)

And one more thing: Mike introduced me to a phrase that has become central to this chapter. Over one of our many barbecue lunches at Stanley's Famous BBQ in Tyler, Texas (a place whose motto is, fittingly, "Be Kind. Have Fun."), he shared an idea that stuck with me: the difference between "have to" and "get to."

We refined that idea together. And it's shaped how I think about motivation, formation, and the role of faculty ever since.

Mike's story isn't just a fun memory or a tribute to a great colleague. It's a window into what this chapter is really about: the power of presence, the importance of culture, and the quiet, daily choices that shape how students experience learning. His instinct to listen, to care, and to reframe challenge as opportunity—that's the heart of the "get-to" mindset. And in a world increasingly shaped by speed, shortcuts, and automation, that mindset is more important than ever.

WHERE FORMATION BEGINS

We live in a world of instant everything.

Students can summon answers in seconds. They can generate essays, solve equations, and summarize readings with a few keystrokes. They can scroll endlessly, swipe effortlessly, and binge perpetually. The digital age has trained them to expect speed, ease, and immediacy.

But formation doesn't work that way.

Formation is slow. It's relational. It's iterative. It requires presence, patience, and perseverance. And in a world shaped by AI and the dopamine loops of digital life, that feels increasingly countercultural.

This is why the "get-to" mindset matters more than ever.

PART III. RELATIONAL AND THEOLOGICAL RESPONSE

It's not just a motivational trick. It's a spiritual posture. It's a way of resisting the cultural tide that says learning is a transaction, not a transformation. It's a way of reclaiming education as a calling, not a chore.

And faculty are the ones who can model it.

FACULTY AS COUNTER-FORMATIONAL FORCES

In the digital age, students are being formed—whether we like it or not. Their attention is fragmented. Their motivation is extrinsic. Their default mode is "How fast can I get this done?" not "What kind of person am I becoming?"

AI accelerates this. It offers shortcuts that bypass struggle. It rewards output over insight. It tempts students to trade depth for speed, and growth for performance.

But faculty can push back.

When a professor says, "This is hard—and that's why it matters," they are resisting the culture of ease. When they say, "Let's slow down and think about this," they are resisting the culture of speed. When they say, "You get to wrestle with this idea," they are resisting the culture of passivity.

In short, they are forming students in a different direction.

THE BIG SIX, REFRAMED FOR THE DIGITAL AGE

In 2014, Gallup, Purdue University, and the Lumina Foundation conducted a landmark study to identify what makes college "worth it."[1] They found that six specific experiences—three relational, three practical and applied—were strongly correlated with long-term well-being and workplace engagement. This work has been repeated several times in the intervening years.

These six experiences map directly onto the t-shaped engineer model. The first three are about relational breadth. The next three are about technical depth applied in real-world contexts. However, something is missing—something profound. This study was secular and missed the third axis of the t-shaped model—the telos for our very existence—the aspect of serving God with our work and helping to build his kingdom.

Even with this piece missing, the roadmap of the Big 6 is helpful as we analyze what is going astray with the current engineering educational

---

1. Gallup, "Great Jobs, Great Lives."

landscape. Sadly, only 3% of alumni surveyed said they had experienced all six, notwithstanding the important missing element.

That's a challenge. But it's also an opportunity. We need to reach more students, *and* add the missing piece.

But in the age of AI, these experiences take on new urgency:

Relational Experiences

1. A professor who makes you excited to learn → counters apathy and algorithmic boredom

2. A professor who cares about you as a person → counters isolation and digital disconnection

3. An encouraging mentor → counters the illusion that AI can replace human guidance

Practical and Applied Experiences

4. A long-term project → counters the culture of instant gratification

5. An internship → counters the abstraction of AI-generated work

6. Active involvement in extracurriculars → counters the passivity of screen-based life

These aren't just nice-to-haves. They are antidotes to the spiritual and cognitive erosion of the digital age.

In the age of AI, where efficiency is prized and shortcuts are plentiful, the posture with which students approach learning matters more than ever. Are they grinding through assignments because they have to—or are they engaging with curiosity and purpose because they get to?

This shift in mindset—from obligation to vocation—is not just motivational. It's formational. And faculty are at the heart of it.

The fifth initiative in our roadmap that I'll describe in detail soon is deceptively simple: create a culture where students see learning as a privilege, not a burden. But culture doesn't change by accident. It changes through people. And in higher education, no group shapes culture more than faculty.

Faculty set the tone. They model the mindset. They are the ones who can say, "This is hard—and that's why it matters." They are the ones who can reframe a difficult assignment as an opportunity to grow, not just a hoop to jump through.

But how do we know this matters? Let's look at the data for my home institution.

FACULTY CARE: THE LETOURNEAU EXAMPLE

At our university, we've tried to take this seriously. We surveyed students about how much they feel cared for—by their peers and by their professors—across four dimensions:

- Care for them as a person
- Care for their academic progress
- Care for their career success
- Care for their spiritual growth

The results were striking. Across over 500 respondents, students rated their peers' care at around 4.0 on a 5-point scale. But they rated their professors' care at 4.5. That's a significant difference. It means students know their professors care—and that care matters.

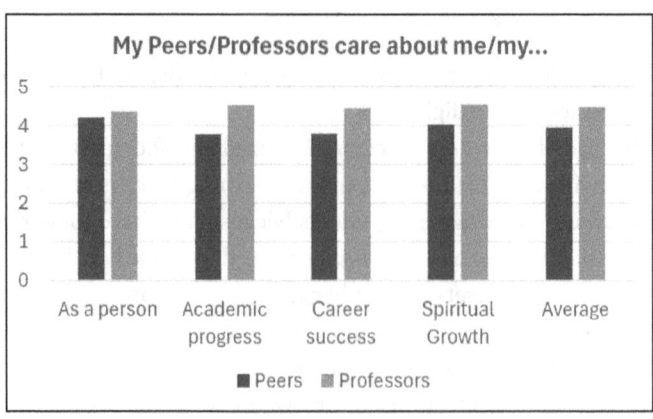

SEET Faculty Care for Students (Student-rated)

In a smaller follow-up alumni survey, we asked about the relative impact of peers, professors, and programs. Again, professors stood out. People mattered more than programs, since peer interactions were also highly rated. Relationships mattered more than resources.

Type	Category	Average
PROF	My PROFESSORS cared about my faith	4.8
PEER	Discussion of meaning and purpose with my PEERS	4.8
PROF	Personal relationships with PROFESSORS	4.7
PROF	My PROFESSORS were excited about my faith	4.7
PEER	Spending time with PEERS	4.7
PROF	A PROFESSOR mentored me about my faith	4.6
PEER	Discussing religion and spirituality with my PROFESSORS	4.5
PROF	Directed prayer with PROFESSORS	4.4
PROG	Classes tied to God's purpose	4.4
PROF	Discussing meaning and purpose with my PROFESSORS	4.4
PROG	Working on a long-term project	4.3
PROG	Activities in the dormitory	4.3
PROG	Internship	4.2
PROG	Theology Core	4.2
PROG	Devotionals	4.1
PROG	Chapel	4.1
PROG	Campus life activities	3.8

Alumni Survey Results

A third study—the Thriving Survey from Fall 2024—confirmed this. Compared to national benchmarks, our students scored lower on peer-related questions (friendship, loneliness, support networks), but significantly higher on professor-related questions. The difference was statistically significant ($p = 0.001$ for professors, $p = 0.041$ for peers). In the table below the data is on a six point scale, with the Benchmark comprised of data from a nationally representative subset of Universities.

PART III. RELATIONAL AND THEOLOGICAL RESPONSE

Peer Questions	Benchmark	LETU	Delta
Making friends	3.21	3.06	-0.15
Friends care	5.03	4.95	-0.08
Number of friends	3.63	3.58	-0.05
Content with friends	4.77	4.58	-0.19
Often lonely	3.88	3.78	-0.10
Hard to make friends	4.06	4.13	0.07
Interactions with other students on campus	4.83	4.80	-0.03
Interactions with different ethnicities	4.87	4.92	0.05
College peers impacts faith	4.91	4.85	-0.06
		Average Delta	-0.06
Faculty/Staff Questions	**Benchmark**	**LETU**	**Delta**
Fac/staff/admin acts consistent with mission	5.01	5.23	0.22
Amount of contact with professors	4.85	4.93	0.08
Academic advising	4.65	4.73	0.08
Quality of interaction with profs	4.92	5.09	0.17
Level of compassion	5.08	5.12	0.04
Connected with instructors outside of class	3.87	4.12	0.25
Interacted socially outside of class	2.99	3.27	0.28
		Average Delta	0.16

Thriving Data

Interpreting this data, I come to two conclusions. First, as a STEM focused institution (with more STEM students as a proportion of the student body than MIT), perhaps the stereotype is somewhat true. Perhaps our STEM students (primarily engineering) do find it a bit more difficult to make friends and connect to people. This is a confirmation for the need for emphasis on cultivating relational skills in the t-shaped engineer model. And second, the anchors of positive formation and transformation at our institution seem to be the faculty. In other words: professors matter. A lot.

WHY THIS MATTERS FOR FORMATION

In a world shaped by AI, students can get answers from machines. But they can't get care. They can't get mentorship. They can't get the kind of presence that says, "You matter. Your work matters. Let's walk this road together."

That's what faculty offer. And that's why cultivating a "get-to" culture isn't just about motivation—it's about creating an ecosystem that fosters growth and the development of wisdom.

When students feel seen, supported, and challenged by faculty who care, they are more likely to:

- Persevere through difficulty
- Engage deeply with their work
- Connect their learning to a larger purpose
- Flourish—not just succeed

This is the heart of the t-shaped engineer: not just technically excellent, but relationally grounded and theologically formed.

So, what is our appropriate response—how can we make this a concrete actions step to transform the lives of more students, and do so in more impactful more spiritual ways?

INITIATIVE 5: CULTIVATING A "GET-TO" CULTURE

This initiative appears last in the roadmap not because it is least important, but because it is most essential. Without a culture that frames learning as a calling rather than a chore, the other initiatives risk becoming techniques rather than transformation. Faculty development, AI literacy, ethical discernment, and curricular innovation all depend on a shared posture—a deep, communal belief that education is a gift. If this culture takes root, the rest of the dominoes are more likely to fall. But without it, even the best strategies may fail to form the kind of engineers—and people—we hope to send into the world.

In an age of automation, it is easy for students to see learning as transactional: a series of tasks to complete, hoops to jump through, or boxes to check. But Christian education calls us to something deeper. Learning is not a burden to endure—it is a gift to steward. A "get-to" mindset reframes education as a response to calling, not compulsion.

This initiative addresses the motivational crisis at the heart of the digital age. It draws on research in positive psychology, which shows that gratitude, autonomy, and meaning are key drivers of sustained engagement.[2] It also aligns with theological anthropology: we are not machines

2. Seligman, *Flourish*.

PART III. RELATIONAL AND THEOLOGICAL RESPONSE

to be optimized, but image-bearers called to love God with our minds (Mark 12:30).

Goal: Shift the mindset from obligation to vocation.

Rationale: Students who see learning as a "get-to" are more likely to persevere through difficulty, engage deeply, and connect their studies to a larger purpose. Faculty who model this mindset help cultivate a culture of joy, resilience, and worshipful curiosity.

Action Steps:

- Deliver a "Welcome Back" lecture at the start of each semester that frames learning as a calling. Include testimonies from faculty and alumni. Again I note that this fits with my University culture. Your institution might deliver a different kind of anchoring, orienting, and impactful experience focused on this goal and rationale.

- Integrate "get-to" language into syllabi, advising, and classroom rituals. For example: "We get to wrestle with this problem because it matters for human flourishing."

- Encourage faculty to redesign at least one assignment per course to reflect a "get-to" framing—emphasizing creativity, relevance, or service.

- Send mid-semester encouragements to faculty with sample affirming phrases that they can use with students: "It's okay—this is supposed to be hard. That means you're learning."

CULTURE IS THE CURRICULUM

Every time I've served on a hiring committee, I've been first in line to volunteer. Not because I love paperwork. Not because I enjoy long interviews. But because I've learned something the hard way: one bad hire can shape a culture for years.

Culture is fragile. And powerful. It's the air students breathe. The tone faculty set. The difference between "have-to" and "get-to."

There's a book I often think about—*The No Asshole Rule* by Robert Sutton.[3] The title is off-putting and blunt, but the insight is sharp: toxic people don't

3. Sutton, *The No Asshole Rule*.

FROM 'HAVE-TO' TO 'GET-TO'—FACULTY AT THE CENTER

just make work unpleasant. They corrode trust. They kill initiative. They shape the hidden curriculum of a place. And once that culture sets in, it's hard to undo.

The quote often attributed to Peter Drucker—"Culture eats strategy for breakfast"—captures this perfectly. Whether or not Drucker actually said it, the truth remains: you can have the best plans, the best programs, the best pedagogy—but if the culture is off, none of it sticks.

Patrick Lencioni has spent his career making the same case. In *The Advantage*, he argues that organizational health—not strategy, finance, or technology—is the greatest advantage any institution can cultivate.[4] Healthy cultures are built on trust, clarity, and shared purpose. In *The Five Dysfunctions of a Team*, he shows how vulnerability, honesty, and alignment are not soft skills—they're survival skills.[5] And in *The 6 Types of Working Genius*, he reminds us that when people are placed in roles that align with their gifts, culture becomes a catalyst for joy, not just productivity.[6]

This is why the "get-to" mindset isn't optional—it's essential. When I present the 2x2 matrix that frames this book, I often pause and say it plainly: if we can't get students to the "get-to" end of the pool, we're dead. The new environment—shaped by AI, distraction, and disconnection—will not allow formation to flourish in a culture of obligation. If we don't shift the posture, we won't shift the outcome.

That's why Initiative 5 matters. It's not a policy. It's a posture. A shared commitment to create a culture where learning is a gift, not a grind. Where students don't just survive—they flourish. Where faculty don't just deliver content—they model calling.

Because in the end, students don't just remember what we taught.

They remember how it felt to be here.

And that feeling? That's culture.

And culture shapes character.

---

4. Lencioni, *The Advantage*.
5. Lencioni, *The Five Dysfunctions of a Team*.
6. Lencioni, *The 6 Types of Working Genius*.

PART III. RELATIONAL AND THEOLOGICAL RESPONSE

A CALL TO FACULTY

If you're a faculty member reading this, here's the invitation: You are not just a content expert. You are a culture maker. You are a mentor. You are a guide.

You don't have to be perfect. You just have to be present.

Ask your students how they're doing. Tell them why the work matters. Share your own struggles and joys. As often as possible let them 'see behind the curtain' to the why behind what you are doing (and honestly self reflect in this space too—is your why good enough? Formational enough?). Model the "get-to" mindset. And trust that your care is not just appreciated—it's transformative.

PART IV

Summation and Vision—
A Call to the Builders

Parts I through III have taken us on a journey—from diagnosis to technical response, and then into the deeper waters of relational and theological formation. We've explored how AI is reshaping not only what students learn, but how they live, relate, and grow. We've proposed a roadmap of initiatives designed to help Christian engineering education respond with clarity, courage, and care.

But this final section is different.

Part IV is not just a conclusion. It is a call. A call to reflect, to synthesize, and to act. It is a space to ask: What have we learned? What questions remain? And how do we move forward—not just as educators or engineers, but as builders of a better world?

Chapter 12 offers a culminating reflection—a synthesis of the book's central themes and a candid look at the challenges still ahead. It revisits the frameworks we've explored and invites us to consider how formation can flourish even in the midst of cultural and technological storms.

Chapter 13 brings the vision to life through the voice of a Christian CEO—someone navigating AI not from the classroom, but from the corner office. His story reminds us that the questions we've explored are not theoretical. They are real. They are urgent. And they are already shaping the future of work, leadership, and witness.

Together, these chapters invite us to step back and see the whole picture. To remember that the goal is not just better pedagogy or smarter tools. It is the formation of wise, grateful, and loving people—engineers who can

PART IV. SUMMATION AND VISION

build not just systems, but communities. Not just products, but purpose. Not just careers, but callings.

This is the moment to gather what we've learned, to name what we still don't know, and to commit ourselves to the work ahead.

Let's build.

CHAPTER 12

Formation in the Storm

SOMETHING TO SAY

As I prepared to interview for my current role as Dean of Engineering and Engineering Technology at "The Christian Polytechnic University," I found myself in a season of deep reflection—and no small amount of anxiety. Was my faith rich enough? Deep enough? Mature enough?

I had come to faith later in life. Thankfully, I'd spent years in a Wesleyan-inspired "Class Meeting" small group, where each week we wrestled with two deceptively simple questions: "How is it with your soul?" and "How has God shown up for you this week?" As a runner, I logged countless miles probing my relationship with God—asking questions, reflecting, forming. In many ways, it felt like preparing to teach a subject: you have to re-learn it yourself, searching for nuance, ensuring your grounding is strong.

It felt like a big ask to become the spiritual head of a school at such a deeply Christian institution. But by the time the interview came, I felt ready.

There was another question, though—one that kept surfacing. As I consulted colleagues, digested articles, read advice columns, all offered the same advice: don't go into the interview with a fully formed vision. Too risky, they said. You'll upset people if you diagnose what's wrong and propose a way forward.

All except one.

PART IV. SUMMATION AND VISION

Joe Boylan (remember him from Chapter 9—crusty, prickly, and wise?) said two things: "Mike, if you don't have something to say, what in the world are you doing?" And "when you get there, *immediately* start trying to get people on the bus to go with you."

So, I studied the university, I studied the school. I thought hard about what it could become. I envisioned the steps we—note the pronoun change —ought to take to get there. I crafted a vision for a job that should be held by a vision caster.

It was the best interview I've ever had. I got the job. I haven't looked back.

Another debt to my dear, departed friend Joe.

Since Day 1, I've been working to build a team and move us toward where we need to go. I hope I'm succeeding.

Why share this?

Because this book has been about that very process: grounding myself in faith, diagnosing a challenge, discerning a path forward, and inviting others to come along.

I hope you will get on the bus with me.

This Chapter is structured to review what we've learned and address some lingering questions.

PART I: WHAT WE'VE LEARNED

Let's go back to the beginning.

We started with a question: *What kind of engineers are we forming?* And a deeper one still: *What kind of people are we becoming in the age of AI?*

We named the cultural moment—marked by distraction, disconnection, and a crisis of meaning. We explored how AI is not just a tool, but a force reshaping how students think, feel, and live.

Reintroducing the 2x2 Matrix: A Compass for the Age of AI

Let's return to the framework that has quietly shaped this entire book: the 2x2 matrix.

It began with two simple questions:

- How should we respond to AI in education?
- How do we help students move from obligation to vocation?

From those questions, two axes emerged:

- **Horizontal axis**: AI-Proofing ⟷ AI-Enhancing
  → Are we resisting AI or integrating it wisely?

- **Vertical axis**: Have-To Learning ⟷ Get-To Learning
  → Are students learning out of compulsion or calling?

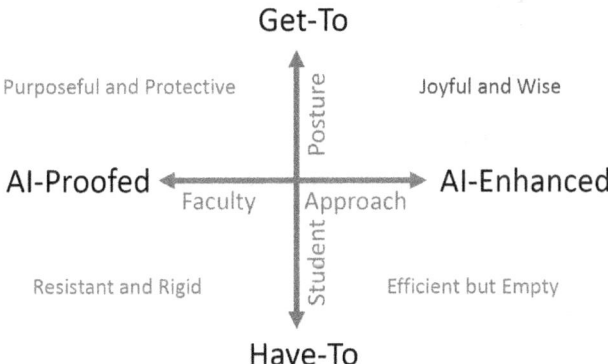

The 2x2 Simplified

These axes form four quadrants—each representing a different posture toward AI and education.
Let's walk through them:

1. **Resistant and Rigid (AI-Proofing + Have-To)**
   This is the "no AI allowed" zone. It's marked by fear, control, and nostalgia. Students feel burdened. Faculty feel defensive. Learning becomes a compliance exercise.

2. **Efficient but Empty (AI-Enhancing + Have-To)**
   Here, AI is used—but only to get things done faster. Students shortcut thinking. Faculty automate grading. The soul of learning is lost in the name of productivity.

3. **Purposeful and Protective (AI-Proofing + Get-To)**
   This quadrant resists AI not out of fear, but out of discernment. It protects sacred spaces of struggle, presence, and formation. It says, "We don't use AI here—not because we can't, but because we shouldn't."

PART IV. SUMMATION AND VISION

4. **Joyful and Wise (AI-Enhancing + Get-To)**
This is often the goal. AI is used as a tool for growth, not a crutch for avoidance. Students are curious, not just compliant. Faculty are guides, not gatekeepers. Learning is a gift, not a grind.

This matrix is more than a diagnostic. It's a compass. It helps us locate where we are—and where we want to go.

And it's not just about AI. It's about helping students become people who can think deeply, love well, and live wisely in a world of machines.

The five initiatives in this book are designed to move us toward that upper-right quadrant. They are not just strategies. They are signposts—pointing toward a new kind of education. One that is not just technically excellent, but spiritually resilient.

At first glance, the two axes of the 2x2 matrix might seem to divide responsibilities:

- The **vertical axis**—from "Have-To" to "Get-To"—appears student-focused. It reflects mindset, motivation, and posture toward learning.

- The **horizontal axis**—from "AI-Proofing" to "AI-Enhancing"—seems faculty-driven. It reflects course design, institutional policy, and pedagogical philosophy.

But this is a false separation.

In truth, both axes are shared. Formation is never a solo act. It is always relational. Always communal. Always t-shaped.

Faculty shape the "Get-To" mindset not just by what they say, but by what they assign. If we ask students to compute logarithms by hand with a slide rule in 2025, we are not inviting them into wonder—we are reinforcing drudgery. If we design assignments that feel like busywork, we cannot expect students to experience learning as a gift.

Likewise, students shape the "AI-Proofing vs. AI-Enhancing" axis by how they engage. If they use AI to bypass thinking, they undermine the very growth and development we hope to cultivate. But if they use it to explore, reflect, and iterate, they elevate the learning experience for everyone. Student integrity will be central.

This is the heart of the t-shaped model: formation is not something we do to students. It is something we do with them.

The 2x2 matrix is not a map of roles. It is a map of relationships. It reminds us that the classroom is not a transaction. It is a covenant. A shared space of becoming.

The Heart of the Matter—the t-Shaped Engineer

If the 2x2 matrix is the compass, then the t-shaped engineer is the destination.

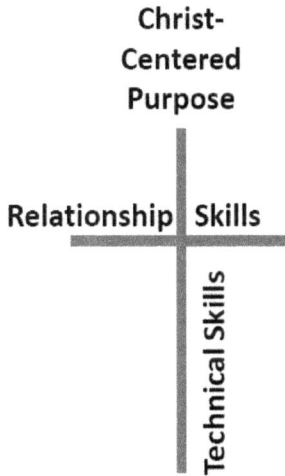

Once Again, the t-shaped engineer

Throughout this book, we've returned again and again to this model—not as a clever metaphor, but as a vision for what Christian engineering education can become.

The t-shaped engineer integrates three essential dimensions:

- **Technical Depth**
  → Mastery of engineering fundamentals, tools, and methods. The ability to design, build, and solve with excellence.

- **Relational Breadth**
  → The capacity to collaborate, communicate, and lead with empathy. The ability to work well with others, across disciplines and differences.

- **Christ-Centered Purpose**

PART IV. SUMMATION AND VISION

→ A vocational pursuit rooted in the love of God and neighbor. The ability to see engineering not just as a job, but as a calling.

This model is shaped like a lowercase "t" for a reason. It is a cross. A reminder that our work is not neutral. It is spiritual. It is relational. It is redemptive.

It is also a rebuke to the dominant models of engineering education that prioritize technical mastery while neglecting meaning and purpose. The t-shaped engineer is not just a better employee. They are a better human. A more whole person. A more faithful steward.

And this model is not just for students. It is for faculty. For institutions. For all of us.

- When faculty teach with clarity and care, they model relational breadth.
- When they frame learning as a calling, they root engineering in faith.
- When they resist the temptation to outsource formation to machines, they protect the sacred space of struggle, presence, and growth.

Likewise, when students engage with curiosity, humility, and perseverance, they are not just learning—they are becoming.

And in the age of AI, this model becomes even more urgent.

Because AI can replicate technical depth. It can even simulate relational cues. But it cannot ground us in purpose. It cannot teach us to love. It cannot form us in the image of Christ.

Only people can do that. Only communities can do that. Only our walk with Jesus can do that.

That is the heart of this book. That is the heart of Christian engineering education. That is the heart of the t-shaped engineer.

The Five Initiatives as Roadmap: From Vision to Practice

If the t-shaped engineer is the destination, and the 2x2 matrix is the compass, then this roadmap is the path forward.

As I've researched and written this book, I've encountered many compelling voices arguing that AI demands a response—that it will change us, that it will be transformative, that it will force us to reexamine what it means to be human. These are important insights. But what I found lacking—almost universally—were concrete, actionable steps. Few offered a way forward. Fewer still offered a path grounded in formation, community, and hope.

This roadmap is meant to fill that gap.

Throughout this book, we've argued that Christian engineering education must be more than technically excellent—it must be spiritually resilient, relationally rich, and theologically grounded. But how do we get there?

These five initiatives are not theoretical. They are practical, actionable, and already being piloted in real classrooms. They are designed to move institutions, faculty, and students toward the upper-right quadrant of the 2x2 matrix—where AI is used wisely, and learning is experienced as a gift. They are structured to fit my University's rhythms, climate and culture. The Chapters where they are introduced provide the goals, rationale and detailed structure to allow them to be easily modified for many different types of institutions. With a few simple changes (i.e. lunch-and-learn to workshop or training module, workshop to student peer group or learning community), I'm confident that the goals, rationale and structure will lead to something concrete, actionable and impactful at many other institutions. Let's revisit them one final time, together:

1. Embed Critical AI Engagement in the Curriculum

Use AI not just to complete tasks, but to reflect, critique, and grow. This initiative invites students to engage AI with discernment. It's not enough to use the tools—we must teach students to ask: What did the AI get right? What did it miss? What does this mean for how I think, learn, and lead?

2. Host a Faculty Lunch-and-Learn on PERMA

Equip faculty to foster environments of purpose, joy, and resilience. Faculty are not just content experts—they are culture-makers. This initiative helps them reflect on their own flourishing and equips them to create classrooms where students can thrive emotionally, intellectually, and spiritually.

3. Offer a Student Workshop on AI Prompting and Best Practices

Teach students to use AI as a tool for learning, not shortcutting. This hands-on workshop demystifies AI and empowers students to use it well. It

PART IV. SUMMATION AND VISION

teaches them how to prompt, evaluate, and iterate with integrity—so they remain the authors of their own learning.

4. Propose a New General Education Course: AI and Human Flourishing

Create space for theological, ethical, and cultural reflection on AI. This course invites students to wrestle with the big questions: What does it mean to be human in an age of machines? How do we use technology in ways that honor God and serve others? It's not just about literacy—it's about wisdom.

5. Establish a "Get-To" Culture Across the School

Reframe learning as a calling, not a chore.
This initiative is about mindset. It's about helping students and faculty alike rediscover the joy of learning. It's about moving from "I have to do this" to "I get to do this"—because learning is a gift, and growth is a privilege.

These five initiatives are not exhaustive. But they are catalytic. They are designed to be implemented, adapted, and refined. They are not the end of the journey—they are the beginning of a new kind of formation.

One that is slower. Deeper. More human. More holy.

PART II: WHAT WE HAVEN'T ANSWERED (YET)

This book has offered a vision, a model, and a roadmap. But it would be dishonest to pretend we've solved everything. In fact, the deeper we go, the more questions emerge—questions that are not just logistical, but philosophical, pedagogical, and spiritual.

These are some of the questions we must now face together.

What Do We Remove to Make Room for AI?

If AI can now perform tasks that once required hours of human effort—solving equations, generating code, summarizing texts—then what do we no longer need to teach in the same way? What becomes obsolete, or at least optional?

This is not a call to lower standards. It's a call to reallocate attention. If AI can handle the mechanical, we must double down on the meaningful. We must ask: What is worth our students' time, effort, and presence?

What Becomes Possible?

The flip side of subtraction is expansion. If we remove the rote, what can we now include?

- More time for reflection and iteration
- More space for interdisciplinary exploration
- More opportunities for mentorship, community, and spiritual formation
- More room for students to wrestle with purpose, not just performance

AI doesn't just compress the curriculum. It can expand the imagination—if we let it.

What Is Essential Knowledge?

This is the heart of the matter. What must students still know, even if AI can do it faster?

- They must know how to think—critically, ethically, theologically.
- They must know how to learn—curiously, humbly, persistently.
- They must know how to relate—with empathy, clarity, and courage.
- They must know who they are—and whose they are.

These are not just academic outcomes, they are essential to character and spiritual development.

The Perfect Storm

The impact of a confluence of factors will undoubtedly cause further change, consternation and opportunity:

PART IV. SUMMATION AND VISION

1. A Generation Shaped by Anxiety and Digital Fatigue

Gen Z students are arriving on campus with unprecedented levels of anxiety, loneliness, and mental health challenges. They are digitally connected but relationally starved. They are fluent in screens but often fragile in spirit. The classroom must now be a place of healing as much as it is a place of learning.

2. A Technological Tsunami

AI is not just a new tool—it is a new context. It is changing how students learn, how faculty teach, and how institutions operate. It is accelerating the pace of change and raising existential questions about what education is for and what it means to be human.

3. A Crisis of Confidence in Higher Education

Public trust in the value of a college degree is eroding. Rising costs, student debt, and questions about return on investment have led many families to reconsider whether college is worth it. For Christian institutions, the challenge is even greater: to demonstrate not only academic excellence but also spiritual and moral clarity.

4. A Decline in Christian Affiliation

The percentage of U.S. adults identifying as Christian has dropped from 75% to 63% in just over a decade.[1] Nearly 30% now identify as religiously unaffiliated. This trend is no longer limited to mainline denominations—it is affecting evangelical communities as well. For Christian universities, this is not just a cultural shift. It is a missional crisis.

5. The Demographic Cliff

Perhaps the most sobering trend is the one that's already baked into the numbers: the demographic cliff. Due to declining birthrates during the Great Recession, the number of high school graduates in the U.S. is

---

1. Pew Research Center, *Decline of Christianity in the U.S.*.

projected to drop sharply starting in the mid-to-late 2020s. While some regions may be somewhat insulated compared to others, regional universities and faith-based institutions are still likely to feel the impact.

And it's not just fewer students—it's also fewer students choosing college at all. The percentage of high school graduates who immediately enroll in a four-year college has declined from 46% in 2016 to 43% in 2021, and the trend appears to be continuing downward.

This is not a temporary dip. It is a structural shift. And it will not affect all institutions equally. Elite universities may weather the storm. But for mission-driven, tuition-dependent schools like mine—and for the broader ecosystem of Christian higher education—the implications are profound.

Each of these forces is significant on its own. Together, they demand a response that is not just strategic—but spiritual. Not just reactive—but redemptive. This is not a moment for minor tweaks. It is a moment for courage, clarity, and conviction.

A CALL TO THE BUILDERS

To the educators:

You are not just teaching content. You are forming souls. You are not just preparing students for jobs. You are preparing them for eternity. Your presence matters. Your posture matters. Your faithfulness matters.

To the parents:

You are not just raising achievers. You are raising image-bearers. Your children need more than skills. They need wisdom. They need love. They need you.

To the thought leaders:

You are not just shaping policy. You are shaping culture. The future of education will not be decided by algorithms. It will be decided by people with vision, courage, and hope.

PART IV. SUMMATION AND VISION

To all of us:

This is not the end of education. It is the beginning of a new kind of formation. One that is slower, deeper, and more human. One that is rooted in love of God and neighbor. One that sees AI not as a threat, but as a test—a test of what we truly value.

The age of AI is here. But so is the call to form engineers who are wise, grateful, and loving.

Let's answer that call.

CHAPTER 13

The CEO and the Crossroads: A Real World Embodiment

INTRODUCTION: A GENTLE REMINDER

Let me introduce you to another member of the next generation of my personal "Board of Directors"—Mitch Fortner.

Mitch is the CEO of an engineering firm based in our region. He's warm, personable, and a deep thinker. He wrestled early with the implications of LinkedIn and the digital age, recognizing its power to extend the reach of business and influence. He's also been a faithful partner to the academy—volunteering his time for Senior Design reviews, entrepreneurship workshops, and more. Every six weeks or so, we meet for coffee. It's become a rhythm I cherish—a chance to catch up, to listen, and to learn.

I taught for 15 years at a secular institution. Mitch was the one who first nudged me toward LeTourneau. "That would be a great fit for you," he said. He was right.

One of our conversations stands out. I was struggling with something at home. My wife—smart, kind, beautiful, and full of gentle faith—had broken her foot. She needed a lot of help. And while I usually find her "princess moments" charming, this time I was losing patience. I shared all this with Mitch over coffee, expecting maybe a laugh or a sympathetic nod.

Instead, he paused, then said quietly, "Well, you know, Mike... I guess I've just always been lucky. Somehow, I've always known that as a husband, it's simply my job to take care of my wife. That's it. I've never had to struggle with that much. I'm just lucky."

He could have corrected me. He could have lectured me about duty, or selfishness, or gratitude. But he didn't. He just offered a gentle reminder—one I could hear. And it landed. I sat there, stunned. Then I laughed. Sometimes, we need someone to say the thing we already know—but in a way that helps us remember.

That's Mitch.

In our most recent coffee, I mentioned this book. His eyes lit up. "I've been wrestling with this too," he said. "What are we going to do as a company? How can this help us? Where will it cause problems?" He started rolling out ideas—things his company is already trying, testing, implementing.

In this chapter, I sit down with Mitch for a deeper conversation. I want you to hear from someone who's leading in the real world—navigating AI not from the classroom, but from the corner office. I'm hoping he'll offer us all what he offered me that day over coffee: a gentle reminder. About where we're going. And why we're going there.

AN INTERVIEW WITH MITCH FORTNER
[MANAGING PRINCIPAL, PAPE-DAWSON ENGINEERS (FORMERLY CEO, KSA ENGINEERS)]

What follows is a structured conversation with Mitch Fortner, Managing Principal at Pape-Dawson Engineers. His insights offer a real-world embodiment of the themes explored throughout this book. After the interview I'll reflect on the main themes and leave us with some final thoughts.

1. VISION & STRATEGY

"How is AI currently shaping your industry—and how do you see that evolving over the next 3-5 years?"

It's been fascinating to watch, Mike. Three years ago, AI was more of a distant rumble in the AEC industry—something talked about in tech conferences but not felt in day-to-day work. But the rumble has grown louder,

THE CEO AND THE CROSSROADS

and now it's unmistakably close. AI is no longer a theoretical conversation. It's showing up in very real, very practical ways.
I see it taking several forms:

- Reducing the volume of tedious work engineers have historically done
- Acting as a personal assistant—reading, summarizing, drafting
- Serving as a knowledge base and enforcing internal standards
- Accelerating quality assurance
- Generating multiple conceptual design ideas
- Improving speed and resolution of architectural renderings

We're also seeing AI integrated into the design software used by engineers, architects, and construction managers. Larger firms are now building dedicated teams to embed AI directly into their workflows.

As for the next 3 to 5 years? I honestly don't know exactly where we'll be. The pace of change is so fast that even 12 months out feels hard to predict. But I'm certain of this: AI is here to stay, and we can't ignore it. We have to adapt. And just as importantly, we have to be wise.

The **NSPE Code of Ethics for Engineers** reminds us that our first responsibility is to "**hold paramount the safety, health, and welfare of the public.**" That doesn't change just because our tools do. If anything, AI raises the stakes. We must ensure that (1) decisions remain grounded in sound engineering judgment, (2) outcomes still meet codes and safety standards, and (3) efficiency never comes at the expense of public well-being. Our ethical calling hasn't shifted—but the way we live it out has become more complex.

2. ORGANIZATIONAL RESPONSE

"**What are some of the first steps your company has taken to engage with AI—either in operations, client work, or internal processes?**"

Our firm, KSA Engineers, Inc., was recently acquired by **Pape-Dawson Engineers**, headquartered in San Antonio. During the due diligence process, one of the key questions our Board asked was: *What is Pape-Dawson's vision for innovation?* We were encouraged—not only by the clarity of the answer, but by the seriousness of their commitment.

In many ways, I believe innovation—especially around AI—is one of the forces driving consolidation in our industry. Smaller firms will find it

PART IV. SUMMATION AND VISION

increasingly difficult to allocate the resources needed to keep up with the pace of change.

Before the acquisition, KSA had taken some early but intentional steps:

- We created an internal policy around AI use
- We invested in Microsoft Copilot licenses
- We formed a users group to explore and share use cases

We were making good progress—but becoming part of Pape-Dawson has accelerated that journey. PD employs a **Vice President of Innovation, Vanessa McMahan**, who is doing tremendous work. The company is actively investing in LLM applications and developing knowledge management systems. What excites me most is that these efforts aren't just coming from the top—they're emerging in **pockets of innovation throughout the company**. And that culture of curiosity is where meaningful change really starts.

3. LEADERSHIP POSTURE

"As a Christian leader, how do you think about the balance between innovation and caution when it comes to adopting AI?"

That's a big question—and one I think about often. To start, I believe it's vital to remember what AI is—and what it isn't. And just as importantly, to remember what we are as human beings.

To be human is to be moral, relational, spiritual, and alive—not just processors of information, but image-bearers of God. While AI can simulate aspects of intelligence, emotion, or creativity, it lacks soul, conscience, and moral depth. As **C.S. Lewis** once said:

"You don't have a soul. You are a soul. You have a body."

That truth anchors me as a leader.

Imagine two firms. One chooses to hold back, unsure about AI and hesitant to experiment. The other dives in headfirst, eager to gain speed and scale, but without much thought for quality or long-term impact. I don't believe either approach reflects the kind of discernment or stewardship Christian leadership calls us to.

The Bible may not speak directly about AI, but it speaks volumes about wisdom, responsibility, and care for others—especially when we're entrusted with tools that can shape lives. I'm convinced that organizations that fail to innovate will lose their ability to serve and compete. But chasing speed at the expense of judgment and safety is just as dangerous.

So we walk a narrow road. We must innovate—but with our eyes open.

4. ETHICAL TENSIONS

"What are the ethical or spiritual questions that keep you up at night when you think about AI's impact on your company and your people?"

Well, I'll be honest—it doesn't keep me up at night. Not much does. But there are real reasons for concern, and I think about them often.

One of my biggest concerns is how AI will shape *us*—not just what it does, but what it does to the people using it. If you were around before social media, it's easy to see how it's affected attention, relationships, and the way we think. AI could have an even deeper impact.

I worry about what we might lose:

- Critical thinking
- Writing ability
- The habit of deep reading
- Human empathy and ethical reflection

I think about a world where my AI sends a sterile message to your AI, which generates a sterile reply—without either of us really engaging the issue at hand. That may be efficient. But it's not very human.

And it's not just the workplace. I imagine walking into a medical clinic and being greeted by a kiosk that draws my blood and delivers a diagnosis in a robotic voice. That might be fast. But it's not care.

I'm not against the tool. I appreciate what AI can do. But I don't want us to lose the **human touch**—the compassion, the empathy, the ethical lens we apply when we interact with one another. That's a real concern of mine.

5. FORMATION & CULTURE

"How do you think AI is shaping the habits, mindset, or character of your employees—and what are you doing to respond?"

Honestly, I don't think we're far enough into widespread AI adoption for it to have profoundly reshaped our people—at least not yet. Most of the effects I see right now are still on the surface: time savings, formatting help, research shortcuts. But deeper change takes longer to set in.

That said, I'm hopeful. If we use AI wisely, it could help relieve some of the burnout that's common in our professions. Engineers and architects often carry a heavy load of repetitive, time-consuming tasks. If AI can take some of that off their plates, it might free up space to focus on what matters most: long-term planning, deeper thinking, team development, and client relationships.

We're still in the early stages, but we're watching closely. My hope is that AI doesn't just make us faster—it makes us **healthier, more thoughtful, and more human** in how we work.

6. TALENT & HIRING

"What are you looking for in new hires today that might be different from five years ago—especially in light of AI?"

Many of the traits we've always looked for still matter most: personal responsibility, sound judgment, the ability to learn, and strong communication—both written and verbal.

What's changed is the environment those traits are being applied in. Today, we also value people who are **technologically curious**—who know how to use tools like AI to innovate, spot inefficiencies, or improve the way we work. You don't need to be a coder. But you do need to be able to **adapt, learn quickly**, and ask good questions. In a world shaped by AI, those who thrive won't just know how to use the tools. They'll know how to lead through the change.

7. ENGINEERING EDUCATION

"If you could speak directly to Christian engineering educators, what would you encourage them to do more of—or differently—to prepare students for this new world?"

I was genuinely excited to read the draft of this book, Mike. I think you've captured exactly what we're hoping for in the next generation of engineers. We need students to graduate with strong technical skills *and* strong people skills—a good balance between competence and character.

One area I believe deserves special attention now is helping students learn to use **AI as a tool**, not a crutch. AI shouldn't replace good judgment, clear communication, or deep thinking—but it can enhance all of those when used wisely. I'd love to see colleges train students to use it thoughtfully for research, brainstorming, writing support, even as a kind of extended memory. It's not about outsourcing their thinking—it's about sharpening it.

Christian universities are uniquely positioned to lead here. You can help students understand not just how to use AI, but how to use it **ethically, creatively,** and **responsibly**—with humility, curiosity, and a deep sense of calling.

8. FAITH & LEADERSHIP

"How does your faith shape the way you lead in this moment of technological change?"

Full disclosure: I'm 63 years old as I write this. And over the course of my life, I've come to understand that the Christian journey is a marathon, not a sprint. Spiritual formation happens slowly—and that's certainly been true in my own life. One conviction that has grown stronger with time is what **Abraham Kuyper** expressed in his doctrine of **Sphere Sovereignty:**

"There is not a square inch in the whole domain of our human existence over which Christ, who is sovereign over all, does not cry: 'Mine!'"

That includes how we lead companies—and how we respond to technological change.

I also believe the Bible is the inspired, unchanging, authoritative, and sufficient Word of God. That belief shapes everything—from the way I think about innovation to the way I think about people. It reminds me that our approach to leadership must be rooted in compassion, wisdom, and truth.

Jesus said the greatest commandment is to love God with all our heart, soul, and mind, and to love our neighbor as ourselves. And Paul told the Colossians to "work heartily, as unto the Lord." That perspective transforms how we lead. Even in the face of disruption, our work carries purpose—and our people deserve care.

9. HOPE & OPPORTUNITY

"What excites you most about the future of engineering and technology—especially for Christians in the field?"

Professionals in the AEC industry have always done life-changing work. One of the first projects I ever designed was a water standpipe for

PART IV. SUMMATION AND VISION

the City of Tatum, Texas. It wasn't glamorous—but it mattered. It provided water pressure and fire protection to a part of town that needed it. Nearly 40 years later, that standpipe is still there—still doing what we built it to do.

And every time I drive past it on Highway 149, I feel a quiet sense of pride and gratitude. Not because it's a monumental structure, but because it helped people.

That's what excites me most about the future: watching young engineers step into meaningful work. Designing systems, structures, and spaces that improve lives.

For Christians in the field, this is sacred work. It's a calling. We get to bring order out of chaos. To serve the common good. To reflect God's character in how we design, how we lead, and how we care for others. That's a good reason to get out of bed every morning.

10. A GENTLE REMINDER

"If you could offer one gentle reminder to the next generation of engineers, what would it be?"

When I sit with engineering students today, I like to remind them that they're not just choosing a way to make a living—they're choosing a way to make a life. A life of service to others.

My hope for the next generation of engineers is that they enjoy the journey, and that they look carefully for the deeper meaning in the work they do. The projects may come and go, but the purpose can last a lifetime.

And just as importantly, I hope they live balanced lives—giving time and priority to their families, their churches, and their friendships. Those are the things that will matter most in the end.

WHAT WE HEAR: OUR KEY THEMES

Mitch Fortner's voice in this chapter is not just insightful—it's deeply affirming. His words echo the heartbeat of this book: that engineering is not merely a technical pursuit, but a vocational one. That AI is not the enemy, but a tool. And that leadership, rightly exercised, is a form of formation.

AI as Tool, Not Telos

Mitch reminds us that AI is powerful—but it is not ultimate. It can accelerate workflows, reduce burnout, and enhance creativity. But it cannot replace discernment, empathy, or moral judgment. It is a tool to be stewarded, not a telos to be pursued. This distinction is critical. When AI becomes the goal, we risk hollowing out the very formation we seek. But when it is used wisely, it can support the sacred work of becoming.

Leadership as Formation

Throughout the interview, Mitch models a posture of leadership that is pastoral, not just professional. He speaks with humility, clarity, and care. He names the ethical tensions without panic, and the opportunities without hype. His leadership is not reactive—it is rooted. And that rooting comes from faith, from Scripture, and from a deep sense of calling. This is the kind of leadership our students need to see—and become.

Engineering as Sacred Work

The story of the standpipe in Tatum, Texas is emblematic. It's not flashy. It's not disruptive. But it's faithful. It serves. It lasts. Mitch's quiet pride in that project is a reminder that engineering, when done well, is an act of love. It brings order out of chaos. It protects. It provides. It reflects the character of God. This is the telos of engineering—not just to build, but to bless.

The "Get-To" Mindset in Practice

Mitch's gentle reminder to students—that they're choosing a way to make a life, not just a living—is a perfect embodiment of the "get-to" mindset. It reframes education as a privilege, not a burden. It invites students to see their work as worship, their learning as love, and their vocation as service. This mindset is not just motivational—it's formational. And Mitch lives it.

PART IV. SUMMATION AND VISION

The t-Shaped Engineer Embodied

In Mitch, we see the t-shaped engineer come to life. He speaks with technical fluency, relational wisdom, and theological depth. He leads with integrity, mentors with care, and reflects on his own formation with honesty. He is not just a CEO—he is a builder. And his life is a testimony to what this book has argued all along: that engineers, when formed rightly, can shape not just systems, but souls.

OUR GUIDING FRAMEWORKS

Mitch Fortner's interview doesn't just echo the themes of this book—it embodies its frameworks. His leadership posture, organizational strategy, and vocational clarity reflect the very models we've explored throughout these pages.

The 2x2 Matrix: Joyful and Wise in Practice

Mitch lives in the upper-right quadrant. He neither bans AI out of fear nor adopts it blindly for efficiency. Instead, he models discernment—using AI to enhance work while preserving the human touch. His reflections on sterile AI-to-AI communication versus real empathy are a vivid illustration of what happens when we lose sight of formation. Mitch's posture is not just strategic—it's spiritual. He leads with joy, wisdom, and a deep sense of calling.

The t-Shaped Engineer: Fully Formed

Mitch's story is a portrait of the t-shaped engineer in action. His technical depth is evident in his understanding of AI's impact on design, quality assurance, and workflow. His relational breadth shines through in his mentoring, his care for employees, and his emphasis on communication and empathy. And his theological grounding is unmistakable—anchored in Kuyper's Sphere Sovereignty, shaped by Scripture, and expressed through a life of service. Mitch doesn't just talk about formation—he lives it.

The Five Strategic Initiatives: Already in Motion

Mitch's firm is already walking the path this book lays out. They've embedded AI into their workflows (Initiative 1), cultivated a culture of curiosity and innovation (Initiative 5), and are exploring ethical frameworks for responsible use (Initiative 4). His emphasis on mentoring, discernment, and vocational clarity aligns with the goals of faculty development (Initiative 2) and student formation (Initiative 3). In many ways, Pape-Dawson Engineers is a case study in what happens when these initiatives take root.

ONE FINAL CALL:

Mitch Fortner's words offer more than insight—they offer a summons. His gentle reminder to students, his theological grounding in Kuyper's sovereignty, and his vocational clarity all converge into a call for action. Not just for engineers, but for educators, institutions, and leaders across the Christian academy.

To Educators:

You are not just teaching content—you are forming character. Mitch's reflections affirm what you already know: that students need technical depth, yes, but they also need relational wisdom and theological grounding. They need mentors who model discernment, who ask good questions, and who walk the narrow road between innovation and integrity. You are those mentors. Your posture matters. Your presence matters. Your faithfulness matters.

To Students:

You are not just preparing for a job—you are preparing for a life. Mitch's reminder is clear: engineering is a way to serve, to bless, to build. It is sacred work. Don't settle for shortcuts. Don't outsource your thinking. Use AI wisely, but never let it replace the slow, sacred work of becoming. Look for meaning in your projects. Look for joy in your growth. And look for balance—in your work, your relationships, and your walk with God.

PART IV. SUMMATION AND VISION

To Institutions:

You are not just delivering degrees—you are shaping culture. Mitch's firm is already living out many of the initiatives this book proposes. But culture doesn't change by accident. It changes through intentionality, through leadership, and through a shared commitment to formation. Build environments where curiosity is cultivated, where discernment is modeled, and where students are invited to see their work as worship. The age of AI demands clarity, courage, and care. You have the opportunity—and the responsibility—to lead.

This is the moment. The cultural storm is real. The technological shift is accelerating. But the call remains the same: to form engineers who are wise, grateful, and loving. To build not just systems, but communities. Not just careers, but callings. Not just outputs, but offerings.

Let's answer that call.

CLOSING WITH HOPE

We began this book with a question: *What kind of engineers are we forming?* And a deeper one still: *What kind of people are we becoming in the age of AI?*

We've walked through diagnosis, response, and vision. We've named the cultural storm—distraction, disconnection, and the erosion of meaning. We've explored how AI is reshaping not just what students learn, but how they live, relate, and grow. And we've proposed a path forward—one marked by technical depth, relational breadth, and Christ-centered purpose.

But here, at the end, Mitch Fortner offers us something more: a quiet, confident hope.

Hope that engineering can still be sacred.

Hope that leadership can still be wise.

Hope that technology, when stewarded well, can serve—not supplant—human flourishing.

His gentle reminder is the perfect benediction: *You're not just choosing a way to make a living—you're choosing a way to make a life.* A life of service. A life of meaning. A life of balance and joy.

This is the vision. Not just for students, but for all of us. That our work would reflect the character of Christ. That our classrooms would become spaces of formation, not just instruction. That our institutions would model discernment, courage, and care. And that our graduates would go out into the world not just ready to build—but ready to bless.

Because in the end, engineering is not just about solving problems. It's about serving people. It's about loving our neighbor. It's about participating in God's redemptive work in the world.

And that is an awfully good reason to do what we do.

Let's build.

Epilogue: What Are We Building?

MIKE MULLIGAN

I keep three books on my desk at all times: *The Reason for God* (Tim Keller), *The Way Things Work* (David Macaulay), and *Mike Mulligan and His Steam Shovel* (Virginia Lee Burton).[1][2] I'm literally looking at them right now as I type this (thank you, 7th grade typing class, for teaching me to type without looking!).

One of these might seem like it doesn't belong. For now, let me give you a little context.

For those unfamiliar, Mike Mulligan is a steam shovel operator, and Mary Anne is his beloved machine. Together, they've built highways, airports, and canals. But as newer machines replace steam shovels, Mike and Mary Anne take on one final job—digging the cellar for a new town hall. They promise to finish in a single day, hurrying to prove their worth. And, as Burton writes, [Mike] always said that she could dig as much in a day as a hundred men could dig in a week, but he had never been quite sure that this was true." It's a story of grit, loyalty, and transformation.

Perhaps no story—other than the biblical narrative—has resonated more in my life than *Mike Mulligan*. I remember it from childhood. The illustrations were beautiful—something about the artist's technique and vision just captivated me. And I loved Mary Anne, just like Mike Mulligan

---

1. Macaulay, *The Way Things Work*.
2. Burton, *Mike Mulligan*.

EPILOGUE: WHAT ARE WE BUILDING?

did. Maybe it had something to do with his name and mine. I guess I'll never know.

I grew up, became a civil engineer, and had children of my own. I read *Mike Mulligan* to them when they were small, and they loved it. I loved reading it out loud. There's a rhythm to the story—the action builds, the pace quickens as Mike and Mary Anne race the sun. I got so good at reading it that each time it became a performance.

And as I "wrestled" with this children's book, I noticed something else: how incredibly well it matched the civil engineering profession. Not just in what was happening, but in the deeper meaning embedded in the story.

Mike and Mary Anne work their way through a veritable catalog of civil engineering projects: highways, airports, skyscrapers, canals. It became a teaching tool for me—something I used to build excitement for engineering in young people. The message of sustainability is there too: Mary Anne isn't junked—she's reused, reimagined.

And right in the middle of it all is the power of relationship. Mike loves Mary Anne. And if there's a "bad guy" in the book, Councilman Henry B. Swap, he's literally transformed by the power of that love—ending "with a smile that was not mean at all."

This book had so much in it that I used it as part of an engineering outreach program for elementary school students. I've long thought about writing an academic article on Virginia Lee Burton's works—*The Little House, Katy and the Big Snow*, but especially *Mike Mulligan*.[34]

My office walls are lined with engineering drawings. The one front and center when you walk in? A patent drawing from 1919 of a steam shovel that looks remarkably like Mary Anne. I see it every morning.

But my relationship with the book goes deeper still.

During a crisis moment in my family, my teenage daughters arrived at my house scared and shaken—uprooted by an experience I won't detail here, but one that had real, lasting impact. After we collected ourselves and I hugged them, you might guess what happened next.

We sat on the couch. I snuggled them in. And we read *Mike Mulligan* together again.

They remembered it. And it brought calm. Peace. Love. We left the rest of the world behind for a few minutes, built our own little bubble, and listened as Mike and Mary Anne raced the sun:

3. Burton, *The Little House*.
4. Burton, *Katy*.

EPILOGUE: WHAT ARE WE BUILDING?

"But listen! Bing! Bang! Crash! Slam!
LOUDER AND LOUDER, FASTER AND FASTER.
Then suddenly it was quiet.
Slowly the dirt settled down.
The smoke and steam cleared away, and there was the cellar all finished."

This book has meant a lot to me. It may have sparked something in me as a child that wouldn't be harvested until years later. It became an anchor for a K–12 outreach program—because of its technical content, its relational depth, and its ethical themes. And it became a first step toward healing during a family crisis.

Yes, to me, a story can do all this.

This is the power of story. And in many ways, this story became the blueprint for the one you've just read.

This story has become a metaphor for my life—and for this book.

Mike and Mary Anne are not just characters. They are a vision of vocation. They are a reminder that our work matters—not because it is efficient, but because it is faithful. They are a picture of what it means to love what you do, to work with grit and grace, and to be transformed by relationship.

And they are a reminder that even in the age of machines, the most important thing we build is not the cellar—it's the community around it.

Appendix A

A Bit Further Along the Road to How Generative AI Works

For readers coming here from Chapter 6: welcome! You're among the curious who want to understand not just what AI does, but how it does it. What follows is technical but accessible. In Chapter 6, I outlined a puzzle analogy describing how generative AI works. As we work on a puzzle, the steps were explained in this way:

1. Dumping the Pieces = Training on Massive Data
2. Turning the Pieces Over = Tokenization
3. Finding the Edges = Learning Structure
4. Working on Themes = Semantic Clustering
5. Sorting by Color = Attention Mechanisms
6. Sprint to the Finish = Text Generation

In the interest of narrative clarity, I've removed much of the detail from Chapter 6 regarding how all of these steps work in practice. There are great books out there that explain this well—I recommend *AI Basics* (Elsie Olson) (for curious beginners) and *Artificial Intelligence: A Modern Approach* (Stuart Russell & Peter Norvig) (for a more advanced treatment).[1] Here I'm providing that bit more for those who feel they need to climb the mountain a little further (maybe reaching basecamp—try the other books

---

1. Olson, *AI Basics*; Russell and Norvig, *Artificial Intelligence*.

if you are looking for the summit!). For each step in the analogy, what follows are five additional pieces of information: (1) a further description of the technique, (2) what happens when it goes right, (3) what can go wrong, (4) why the step is powerful, and (5) why the step can lead to misunderstandings. Happy reading!

STEP 1: DUMPING THE PIECES = TRAINING ON MASSIVE DATA

"Open the box. Dump all the pieces on the table."

This is the beginning of everything. In puzzle terms, it's the moment of chaos—when you have all the raw material but no structure. In AI terms, this is the **training phase**.

What's Happening Here

In the training phase, a large language model (LLM) like GPT is exposed to a massive dataset—billions of words from books, articles, websites, code repositories, and more. This is called the **corpus**.

The model doesn't know what any of it means. It doesn't even know what "meaning" is. But it starts to learn patterns—how words tend to follow one another, how sentences are structured, how ideas are expressed.

This is like dumping all the puzzle pieces on the table. The model doesn't yet know how they fit together—but it now has access to everything it will ever use to build.

What Can Go Right

- **Breadth of knowledge**: The model can learn from a wide range of disciplines, styles, and voices.

- **Pattern recognition**: It begins to detect statistical regularities in language—what words tend to appear together, how grammar works, and how ideas flow.

- **Scalability**: The more data it sees, the more nuanced its predictions can become.

What Can Go Wrong

- **Bias in the data**: If the training data contains stereotypes, misinformation, or toxic content, the model will absorb those patterns.
- **Overfitting**: If the model memorizes rather than generalizes, it may parrot back training data instead of generating new insights.
- **Opacity**: We don't always know what's in the training data—or how it's shaping the model's behavior.

Why This Step Is Powerful

This is where the model gains its **breadth**. It's why it can write a Shakespearean sonnet, debug Python code, and summarize a legal contract—all in the same conversation. It has seen enough examples to generalize across domains.

Why This Step Can Be Misleading

It's tempting to think that because the model has "read everything," it understands everything. But it doesn't. It has no comprehension, no beliefs, no grounding in reality. It's just seen a lot of puzzle pieces—and learned which ones tend to go next to each other.

STEP 2: TURNING THE PIECES OVER = TOKENIZATION

"Turn all the pieces face up."
Before you can start solving a puzzle, you need to see what you're working with. That's what tokenization does for AI.

What's Happening Here

Tokenization is the process of breaking down text into smaller units—called **tokens**—that the model can understand. These tokens might be whole words, parts of words, or even punctuation marks.

For example:

APPENDIX A

- "engineering" might become: ["engine," "ering"]
- "AI is cool." might become: ["AI," " is," " cool," "."]

Each token is then mapped to a unique number and embedded into a high-dimensional vector space.

What Can Go Right

- **Efficiency**: Tokenization allows the model to process language in manageable chunks.
- **Flexibility**: It can handle multiple languages, slang, and even code.
- **Compression**: Subword tokenization (like Byte Pair Encoding) helps the model deal with rare or made-up words by breaking them into known parts.

What Can Go Wrong

- **Fragmentation**: Words can be split in unnatural ways, making it harder for the model to capture meaning.
- **Loss of nuance**: Token boundaries don't always align with semantic boundaries. For example, "unbelievable" might be split into "un+believ+able," which loses the holistic sense of the word.
- **Bias in token frequency**: Common words are tokenized more efficiently than rare ones, which can skew the model's attention.

Why This Step Is Powerful

Tokenization is the foundation of everything that follows. It's how the model "sees" language. Without it, the model would be trying to solve a puzzle with the pieces still face down.

Why This Step Can Be Misleading

It's easy to assume that because the model can process language, it understands it. But tokenization is mechanical. It doesn't "know" what a word means—it just knows how to break it into parts and assign numbers.

STEP 3: FINDING THE EDGES = LEARNING STRUCTURE

"Find the corners and edges."
Once the pieces are face up, the next step is to find the ones with straight edges. These give the puzzle its boundaries—its structure. In AI, this is the phase where the model begins to learn the **rules of language**.

What's Happening Here

This is where the model starts to understand how language is organized. It learns:

- **Grammar**: how words are ordered in a sentence.
- **Syntax**: how phrases and clauses are structured.
- **Punctuation**: how meaning is shaped by commas, periods, and question marks.
- **Common patterns**: like subject-verb-object, or how questions are formed.

It's not memorizing rules like a grammar textbook. It's learning them statistically—by seeing them over and over again in the training data.

What Can Go Right

- **Fluent output**: The model can generate grammatically correct, natural-sounding language.
- **Style mimicry**: It can imitate the tone and rhythm of different authors or genres.
- **Cross-linguistic generalization**: It can apply structural patterns across languages, even ones it hasn't seen much of.

APPENDIX A

What Can Go Wrong

- **Surface-level fluency**: The model can sound right while being completely wrong—like a student who writes a beautiful essay that says nothing true.
- **False confidence**: Because the structure is smooth, readers may assume the content is accurate.
- **Overgeneralization**: The model may apply patterns where they don't belong, especially in edge cases or technical writing.

Why This Step Is Powerful

This is what makes the model feel "smart." It's why it can write a coherent paragraph, answer a question, or complete your sentence. It's the scaffolding that holds everything else together.

Why This Step Can Be Misleading

Structure ≠ understanding. The model doesn't know what it's saying—it just knows how sentences are usually built. It's like a puzzle with a perfect frame. . . but the picture inside might be upside down.

STEP 4: WORKING ON THEMES = SEMANTIC CLUSTERING

"Work on themes—someone tackles the sailboat, someone else the pine trees."
Once the frame is in place, we start to make sense of the picture by grouping related pieces. In AI, this is where the model begins to understand **meaning**—not just structure.

What's Happening Here

This is the world of **embeddings**.
Each token (word or subword) is mapped to a vector—a list of numbers—that captures its meaning in context. These vectors live in a

high-dimensional space (often 768 or 1,024 dimensions), where **semantic similarity** is represented by **closeness**.

For example:

- "doctor" and "nurse" will be close together.
- "sailboat" and "ocean" will cluster near each other.
- "justice" and "fairness" will share a neighborhood.

This is how the model begins to "work on themes." It doesn't just know what words look like—it knows how they relate.

What Can Go Right

- **Contextual understanding**: The model can disambiguate words based on context (e.g., "bank" as a riverbank vs. a financial institution).
- **Powerful generalization**: It can make analogies, complete metaphors, and even translate between languages.
- **Transfer learning**: These embeddings can be reused across tasks—classification, summarization, translation, etc.

What Can Go Wrong

- **Bias amplification**: If the training data links "nurse" with "woman" or "criminal" with certain ethnicities, those associations are embedded—literally.
- **False proximity**: Words that appear together often may be close in space, even if they're not truly related (e.g., "explosion" and "celebration" in fireworks contexts).
- **Semantic drift**: Over time, meanings shift. Embeddings trained on old data may miss new usage (e.g., "cloud" in tech vs. weather).

Why This Step Is Powerful

This is where the model starts to feel intelligent. It can answer questions, summarize ideas, and generate coherent thoughts—not because it understands, but because it has mapped meaning into math.

APPENDIX A

Why This Step Can Be Misleading

The model doesn't "know" what anything means. It just knows that certain words tend to appear near each other. It's like working on the sailboat section of a puzzle without knowing what a sailboat is—just that these pieces seem to fit.

STEP 5: SORTING BY COLOR = ATTENTION MECHANISMS

"Sort by color when stuck—all the greenish ones here, the blue ones there."

When the puzzle gets tricky, we don't try every piece—we narrow our focus. We group by color, texture, or pattern to make the next move easier. That's exactly what **attention mechanisms** do in AI.

What's Happening Here

In a transformer model (like GPT), **attention** is the mechanism that decides which parts of the input are most relevant when predicting the next token. Instead of treating every word equally, the model assigns **attention weights**—numerical scores that tell it where to "look" more closely.

For example, in the sentence:

"*The trophy didn't fit in the suitcase because it was too small.*"

The model uses attention to figure out what "it" refers to. Is "it" the trophy or the suitcase? Attention helps the model weigh the context and make a statistically informed guess.

What Can Go Right

- **Context awareness**: The model can track long-range dependencies (e.g., pronouns, references, nested clauses).

- **Disambiguation**: It can resolve ambiguity by focusing on the most relevant parts of the sentence.

- **Parallel processing**: Attention allows the model to process all tokens at once, rather than sequentially—making it fast and scalable.

What Can Go Wrong

- **Misplaced focus:** The model might attend to the wrong part of the input, especially in long or complex prompts.
- **Overconfidence:** It may assign high attention to misleading or irrelevant tokens, leading to plausible-sounding but incorrect output.
- **Computational cost:** Attention mechanisms are powerful but expensive—especially for very long inputs.

Why This Step Is Powerful

Attention is what makes modern AI models so effective. It's the breakthrough that enabled GPT, BERT, and other state-of-the-art systems. Without it, the model would be guessing blindly.

Why This Step Can Be Misleading

Just because the model is "paying attention" doesn't mean it understands. It's sorting by statistical relevance—not by meaning, truth, or importance. It's like grouping puzzle pieces by color without knowing what the picture is.

STEP 6: SPRINT TO THE FINISH = TEXT GENERATION

"Sprint to the finish—the last few pieces fall into place quickly."
Once the puzzle is mostly complete, the last pieces come together fast. You can see the picture. You know what's missing. That's what text generation feels like in a well-trained AI model.

What's Happening Here

This is the **inference phase**—when the model is no longer learning, but generating.

Given a prompt, the model predicts the next token (word or subword) based on everything that came before. Then it predicts the next one. And the next. One token at a time, it builds a response.

APPENDIX A

Each prediction is based on **probability**. The model doesn't "choose" the next word—it samples from a distribution of likely options. The more context it has, the better its guesses.

What Can Go Right

- **Fluent, coherent output:** The model can write essays, poems, code, summaries, and more.
- **Contextual adaptation:** It can match tone, style, and structure to the prompt.
- **Speed and scale:** It can generate pages of content in seconds.

What Can Go Wrong

- **Hallucinations:** If the model makes a wrong guess early on, it may build on that error—confidently and convincingly.
- **Overconfidence:** The model doesn't know when it's wrong. It presents every answer with the same tone of certainty.
- **Loss of grounding:** The model doesn't check facts. It doesn't verify sources. It just predicts what sounds right.

Why This Step Is Powerful

This is where the magic happens. It's what makes AI feel conversational, creative, and even insightful. It's the part users see—and often the part they fall in love with.

Why This Step Can Be Misleading

Because the output is so fluent, it's easy to forget that it's just a series of guesses. The model doesn't know what it's saying. It doesn't care if it's true. It's just trying to finish the puzzle—whether the picture is accurate or not.

Appendix B

AI Initiatives for Formation

This appendix gathers the five strategic initiatives from across the book into one place for ease of reference. Each initiative includes its original description and a few simple tools to support implementation. The goal is not to expand the book, but to make it more useful—for educators, administrators, and anyone seeking to apply the ideas in practice. Each includes the original text from the Chapter in which it appears, plus at least one additional resource (e.g. sample syllabus, grading rubric, workshop outline, etc.). The Appendix concludes with a cross-reference and timeline to aid actual implementation.

INITIATIVE 1: EMBED CRITICAL AI ENGAGEMENT IN THE CURRICULUM (CHAPTER 5)

AI is already in the classroom—whether we acknowledge it or not. Students are using tools like ChatGPT, GitHub Copilot, and Grammarly to complete assignments, debug code, and even generate design ideas. The question is not whether they will use AI, but how—and whether they will do so thoughtfully, ethically, and with theological discernment.

This initiative addresses the growing gap between AI usage and AI understanding. It draws on research in cognitive science and educational technology, which shows that students learn best when they are asked to reflect on their tools, not just use them. It also aligns with Christian formation: wisdom is not just knowing what works, but discerning what is good.

APPENDIX B

Goal: Encourage students to think critically about AI, not just use it.
Rationale: When students engage AI without reflection, they risk becoming passive consumers of machine-generated content. But when they are invited to analyze, critique, and compare AI outputs with their own thinking, they develop metacognition, ethical awareness, and intellectual humility. These are not just academic virtues—they are spiritual ones.

ACTION STEPS:

- Each academic program identifies one course per semester (at a minimum) of a student's journey where students:
  - Use AI to complete a task (e.g., generate code, summarize a technical article, draft a design memo).
  - Compare and critique AI-generated work versus their own.
  - Reflect on the strengths, weaknesses, and ethical implications of AI use.
- Faculty are encouraged to model AI use transparently—demonstrating both its power and its limitations.
- Assignments include structured reflection prompts such as:
  - "What did the AI get right?"
  - "What did it miss?"
  - "How did using AI affect your thinking process?"
  - "Would you trust this output in a real-world engineering context? Why or why not?"

This initiative also supports the "AI-enhancing" quadrant of the 2x2 matrix introduced earlier. It does not seek to eliminate AI from the learning process, but to elevate it—to use AI as a catalyst for deeper learning, not a shortcut around it.

Engineering education has long relied on structured pathways—curricular scaffolding, accreditation standards, and pedagogical models that aim to produce technically competent graduates. But as AI reshapes the landscape, those structures are being tested. The algorithms we've trusted to guide formation may no longer be sufficient. In Chapter 6, we'll go deeper—exploring how AI itself works, what it gets right, what it gets wrong, and how its underlying logic challenges the very foundations of how we teach, learn, and grow.

Additional Materials:

Sample Syllabus Statement

Version 1: Syllabus Statement: AI Use and Formation

In this course, we will engage with artificial intelligence (AI) tools as part of our learning journey. AI is not a shortcut—it is a tool that, when used wisely, can deepen understanding, spark creativity, and support growth. You are encouraged to use AI tools (e.g., ChatGPT, Copilot, Grammarly) for brainstorming, drafting, and exploring ideas, but **you must remain the author of your own work.**

All AI use must be disclosed. If you use AI to assist with any assignment, include a brief note at the end describing how you used it (e.g., "Used ChatGPT to generate initial outline; revised and expanded with personal analysis").

AI use is permitted only when it supports learning, not when it replaces it. Submitting AI-generated work without meaningful engagement or reflection is considered academic dishonesty.

This course is grounded in the belief that learning is a gift, not a grind. You don't just "have to" complete assignments—you "get to" grow. Our goal is to help you become not just a better engineer, but a wiser human.

Version 2: Course Policy on AI Tools:

The integration of AI tools (such as ChatGPT, GPT-4, and other similar technologies) is a required component of this course. Students are expected to utilize these tools to enhance their learning experience, assist in research, and improve their assignments. Assignments will include specific tasks where the use of AI is necessary, and students must demonstrate their ability to effectively and ethically use AI. Proper citation and documentation of AI usage is mandatory. Failure to use AI as instructed will impact the student's grade.

APPENDIX B

Sample 'Ethos for AI'

PREAMBLE

As a part of *the Christian Polytechnic University*, we affirm that artificial intelligence (AI) is neither inherently good nor evil. Like the axe in the hands of a woodsman, AI is a tool—capable of warming homes, clearing forests, or causing harm. AI is also a tool that inherently forms the user, just as the axe calluses the hands, changes musculature, and modifies the user's perspective of the forest. As stewards of creation and educators of future t-shaped engineers, we are called to use this tool wisely, ethically, and redemptively.

1. AI AS A TOOL, NOT A TELOS

We affirm that artificial intelligence, like every major technological advancement before it, is a tool—powerful, but not ultimate. The pen and paper allowed God's Word to be written and preserved. The printing press enabled it to be shared widely. Sailing ships carried it across oceans. Computers helped catalog, cross-reference and search it for deeper study. The internet has allowed for an explosion of global communication and access to Scripture. Each of these tools brought great opportunity—and real risk. So too with AI.

We reject the notion that AI defines what it means to be human. Our identity is not found in algorithms, but in the image of God. We affirm that AI can assist in learning, design, and discovery —but it cannot replace the diligent and sacred work of formation by God. It cannot love, repent, or worship. It cannot ask, "Is this good for human flourishing?"

2. FORMATION OVER EFFICIENCY

We will not sacrifice formation on the altar of efficiency. While AI can accelerate tasks, we believe that struggle, iteration, and presence are essential to learning. We will design learning environments that prioritize growth over shortcuts, wisdom over output, and vocation over convenience.

AI INITIATIVES FOR FORMATION

3. The t-Shaped Engineer in the Age of AI

We live in a time of profound disconnection. The digital age has brought unprecedented access to information—but often at the cost of attention, presence, and purpose. Students arrive in our classrooms digitally fluent but relationally fragile, technically capable but spiritually adrift. In this context, the t-shaped engineer is not just a model—it is a response.

We commit to forming engineers who are:

- **Technically excellent** (vertical depth),
- **Relationally wise** (horizontal breadth),
- **Christ-centered** (upward purpose).

This model is shaped like a lowercase "t"—a cross. It reminds us that engineering is not just about solving problems, but about serving people. Not just about what we can build, but about who we are becoming. In the age of AI, we must form engineers who are not only skilled, but whole—able to lead with wisdom, love, and clarity in a world of accelerating change.

4. Discernment as Discipleship

We will teach students not just how to use AI, but how to think about it. We will cultivate discernment—asking not only "Can we?" but "Should we?" We will frame AI use within a Christian vision of vocation, stewardship, and love of neighbor.

5. Presence Over Simulation

We affirm that real formation happens in real relationships. AI can simulate dialogue, but not mentorship. It can generate feedback, but not care. It can mimic empathy, but not embody it. We will prioritize presence—in the classroom, in advising, and in community.

6. Hopeful, Not Fearful

We will not respond to AI with fear or nostalgia. We will respond with clarity, courage, and hope. We believe that Christian education is uniquely equipped to lead in this moment—not by rejecting technology, but by redeeming its use.

As part of our calling to serve in *every workplace and every nation*, we recognize that AI fluency is no longer optional. It is a core competency for the next generation of engineers, leaders, and problem-solvers.

Employers will expect our graduates to understand and use AI tools with skill, discernment, and integrity. We will not leave them unprepared. We will teach students how AI works, how to prompt it wisely, how to evaluate its output critically, and how to use it ethically.

7. A Call to Stewardship

We call on faculty, staff, students, and leaders to steward AI with integrity. To use it not to bypass formation, but to deepen it.

Conclusion

The invention of calculus, the discovery electromagnetism, the ramifications of the second law of thermodynamics, the creation of the digital computer—each has shaped the way we educate engineers, often allowing us to go further, deeper, and richer, while also introducing new moral and human challenges. So too with AI. Christians are always called to navigate such moments with wisdom and grace—"wise as serpents and innocent as doves" (Matthew 10:16). We will meet this moment by keeping our gaze fixed on the command of Christ: to love God and love our neighbor (Matthew 22:37–39). In doing so, we will form engineers not only ready for the world—but ready to transform it.

INITIATIVE 2: HOST A FACULTY LUNCH-AND-LEARN ON PERMA (CHAPTER 9)

Faculty are not just transmitters of content—they are cultivators of culture. The way they teach, advise, and interact with students shapes not only what students learn, but how they experience learning. In a time when both students and educators are navigating fatigue, uncertainty, and rapid technological change, faculty well-being and motivation are essential to institutional flourishing.

This initiative draws on the **PERMA model** of well-being developed by psychologist Martin Seligman, which identifies five core elements of human flourishing: **Positive Emotion, Engagement, Relationships, Meaning, and Accomplishment.**

Positive Emotion

Positive emotion is more than just feeling happy—it includes hope, gratitude, inspiration, and joy. In the classroom, cultivating positive emotion means creating moments that spark curiosity, celebrate small wins, and remind students (and faculty) why the work matters. It's not about avoiding difficulty, but about framing challenges in a way that invites engagement rather than dread. For Christian educators, this also includes joy rooted in grace—the deep assurance that our worth is not in our performance, but in being loved by God.

Engagement

Engagement is the experience of being fully absorbed in a task—what psychologists call "flow." It happens when students are challenged just enough to stretch, but not so much that they shut down. For faculty, it's the joy of teaching a class that clicks, or mentoring a student who's growing. In a PERMA-informed classroom, engagement is cultivated through active learning, real-world problems, and opportunities for students to use their strengths. It's about designing experiences that invite presence, not just compliance.

Relationships

Relationships are the glue of growth and development. They are the most consistent predictor of student thriving—and faculty thriving too. In the PERMA model, relationships refer to the sense of connection, trust, and belonging that comes from being known and cared for. For Christian educators, this is deeply theological: we are made in the image of a relational God. Classrooms that prioritize relationships—through mentoring, collaboration, and presence—become spaces where students are not just taught, but formed.

APPENDIX B

Meaning

Meaning is about purpose. It's the sense that what we're doing matters—and that it connects to something larger than ourselves. In education, meaning emerges when students see how their work contributes to human flourishing, when they connect their studies to their calling, and when they are invited to wrestle with the "why" behind the "what." For Christian institutions, this is a core strength: we can name the telos. We can say, with clarity and conviction, that our work is part of God's redemptive story.

Accomplishment

Accomplishment is not just about grades or awards—it's about growth. It's the sense of progress, mastery, and resilience that comes from setting goals and working toward them. In a PERMA-informed classroom, accomplishment is celebrated not only in outcomes, but in effort. Students are affirmed for perseverance, iteration, and courage. Faculty, too, need to feel that their work is making a difference—that they are helping students grow, and that their labor is not in vain.

These elements are not only psychologically beneficial—they are pedagogically powerful. When faculty experience purpose and connection in their work, they are more likely to foster those same qualities in their students.

But this initiative is not only about faculty flourishing—it's also about **equipping faculty to create environments where students can flourish.** The PERMA model offers a practical framework for designing classrooms that are not only intellectually rigorous but also emotionally and spiritually supportive. In this way, faculty become agents of growth, shaping spaces where students feel seen, challenged, and inspired.

Goal: Promote well-being and intrinsic motivation among faculty—and equip them to foster the same in their students.

Rationale: Faculty who are flourishing are more likely to create learning environments that are relational, resilient, and reflective. The PERMA model offers a research-based framework for understanding what makes teaching joyful and sustainable. It also resonates with a Christian vision of vocation: that our work is not just productive, but redemptive. When applied to classroom culture, PERMA helps students experience learning as meaningful, connected, and growth-oriented.

ACTION STEPS:

- Organize a lunch-and-learn session introducing the PERMA model, with examples drawn from teaching, mentoring, and curriculum design. Note that lunch-and-learn fits our culture at *my* University. Another institution might pick a faculty workshop, a learning community, an on-line training module, an initiative by a teaching excellence center, or another format that fits *their* culture.
- Invite faculty to reflect on which PERMA elements are most present—and most absent—in their current teaching experience.
- Provide practical strategies for integrating PERMA into classroom culture:
    - **Positive Emotion**: Begin class with a moment of gratitude or curiosity.
    - **Engagement**: Use active learning techniques that invite participation and flow.
    - **Relationships**: Build rapport through office hours, feedback, and shared projects.
    - **Meaning**: Connect course content to real-world impact and Christian vocation.
    - **Accomplishment**: Celebrate progress, not just performance.
- Include a segment on how PERMA can be used to **design assignments, feedback, and classroom rituals** that support student flourishing.
- Follow up with a short survey to assess changes in faculty mindset and morale, as well as perceived impact on student engagement.

Additional Materials:

Sample Lunch-and-Learn Agenda
Lunch-and-Learn Agenda: Cultivating Flourishing through the PERMA Framework
Title: "Flourishing in the Classroom: Using PERMA to Shape Culture and Formation"
Duration: *90 minutes (can be adapted to 60 or 120 minutes)*

APPENDIX B

Welcome & Framing (10 min)

- Opening remarks: "Why flourishing matters in engineering education"
- Brief overview of the t-shaped engineer model and its connection to PERMA

PERMA Overview (15 min)
Quick walkthrough of the five elements:

- **P**ositive Emotion
- **E**ngagement
- **R**elationships
- **M**eaning
- **A**ccomplishment

Faculty Reflection Activity (15 min)

- Prompt: "Which PERMA element is most present in your teaching? Which is most absent?"
- Small group discussion (3–4 per table)
- Optional worksheet or sticky notes for visual mapping

Classroom Strategies (20 min)
Practical examples for each PERMA element:

- P: Start class with a moment of gratitude or curiosity
- E: Use active learning or real-world problems
- R: Build rapport through feedback and mentoring
- M: Connect content to vocation and impact
- A: Celebrate effort and growth, not just grades

Shareable handout with 2–3 strategies per element
Student Voice (10 min)

- Optional: Invite 1–2 students to share what makes a class feel "formational"
- Or read anonymized student quotes from surveys

Closing & Invitation (10 min)

AI INITIATIVES FOR FORMATION

- Recap key takeaways
- Invite faculty to redesign one assignment using PERMA principles
- Optional follow-up: Peer review, showcase, or mini-grant for implementation

Sample Discussion Questions: PERMA and Formation in the Classroom
Opening Reflection

1. Which PERMA element (Positive Emotion, Engagement, Relationships, Meaning, Accomplishment) feels most present in your current teaching practice? Which feels most absent? Why?

2. Think of a recent moment in your classroom that felt "formational" rather than just instructional. What made it different?

Positive Emotion

3. How do you intentionally cultivate joy, curiosity, or gratitude in your classroom? What small practices have made a big difference?

4. What role does humor, storytelling, or celebration play in your teaching? How might these connect to deeper formation?

Engagement

5. When have you seen students enter a "flow" state in your course? What conditions made that possible?

6. How do you balance challenge and support to keep students engaged without overwhelming them?

Relationships

7. What does "relational breadth" look like in your teaching? How do you build trust and connection with students?

8. How do you model presence and care in a digital or AI-enhanced classroom? What's harder now—and what's still possible?

Meaning

9. How do you help students connect course content to their sense of calling or purpose?

10. What theological or vocational themes do you wish students wrestled with more deeply in your discipline?

Accomplishment

11. How do you celebrate growth, not just grades? What practices help students see their progress over time?

12. How do you help students reframe failure as part of formation?

Closing Reflection

13. If you could redesign one assignment or classroom ritual to better reflect PERMA, what would it be?

14. What's one thing you'll try this semester to foster flourishing—for yourself or your students?

INITIATIVE 3: OFFER A STUDENT WORKSHOP ON AI PROMPTING AND BEST PRACTICES (CHAPTER 9)

For many students, AI tools have become a default companion—used late at night, under pressure, and often without guidance. While these tools can support learning, they can also short-circuit it. When students rely on AI to complete tasks without understanding the underlying concepts, they risk becoming passive consumers rather than active thinkers.

This initiative addresses the need for AI literacy that is both technical and ethical. It draws on research in metacognition and self-regulated learning, which shows that students benefit from explicit instruction in how to use tools reflectively and strategically. It also aligns with Christian formation: discernment is not just about what we can do, but what we ought to do.

Goal: Equip students to use AI as a tool for learning, not shortcutting.

Rationale: Students who understand how AI works—and how to work with it—are better prepared for the future of engineering. They are also more likely to retain agency in their learning process. Teaching students how to prompt, evaluate, and iterate with AI fosters intellectual humility, curiosity, and responsibility.

AI INITIATIVES FOR FORMATION

ACTION STEPS:

- Host a hands-on workshop open to all students, ideally early in the semester. While we use the term student workshop here, this initiative can be reframed to fit the culture and rhythms of different institutions. At a research university, it might take the form of a co-curricular seminar series or a "digital fluency" badge program. At a liberal arts college, it could be embedded in a first-year experience course or offered as a faculty-student roundtable. At a community college, it might be a one-credit micro-course or a hands-on lab session during orientation. The format is flexible—the goal is creating an environment where positive growth and change can happen.

- Topics covered:
    - How generative AI models work (brief overview).
    - How to write effective prompts for different tasks (e.g., coding, summarizing, brainstorming).
    - How to evaluate AI responses for accuracy, bias, and depth.
    - How to use AI for ideation, revision, and exploration—not just answers.

- Include discipline-specific examples (e.g., engineering design prompts, technical writing, data analysis).

- Provide a follow-up resource guide with sample prompts, ethical guidelines, and reflection questions.

- Encourage faculty to assign a short reflection after the workshop: "How might you use AI in your learning this semester? What boundaries will you set?"

This initiative supports both axes of the 2x2 matrix: it enhances students' ability to use AI well, while also helping them develop the discernment to know when not to. It reinforces the idea that AI is not a replacement for thinking—but a partner in the process of becoming a thoughtful, ethical engineer.

APPENDIX B

Additional Materials:

Sample Workshop Outline: "Prompting with Purpose: AI as a Tool for Learning and Formation"
Duration: 3 hours
Audience: Undergraduate engineering students (can be adapted for other disciplines)
Workshop Goals:

- Equip students to use AI tools (e.g., ChatGPT, Copilot, Gemini) **ethically, effectively and formationally.**
- Teach **prompting strategies** for ideation, revision, and exploration
- Foster **discernment** around AI use in academic and vocational contexts
- Reinforce the **"get-to" mindset** and the t-shaped engineer model

Agenda
00:00–00:15 Opening Prayer, Welcome & Framing

- Prayer
- Icebreaker: "What's the weirdest or most helpful thing you've asked AI to do?"
- Overview of the workshop goals
- Brief intro to the **t-shaped engineer** and the **2x2 matrix**

00:15–00:45 How AI Works (Accessible Overview)

- Puzzle metaphor recap (from Chapter 6)
- What AI can and can't do
- Hallucinations, limitations, and the illusion of understanding
- Q&A

00:45–01:30 Prompting Strategies for Learning

- **Mini-lecture + live demo**: How to write effective prompts
  - Brainstorming
  - Summarizing
  - Reframing
  - Simulating Socratic dialogue

AI INITIATIVES FOR FORMATION

- **Hands-on activity:** Students try 3 types of prompts on a shared topic
- **Reflection:** What worked? What surprised you?

01:30–01:45 Break (with snacks or lunch)
01:45–02:15 Ethical Use & Disclosure

- Case studies: Good vs. problematic AI use
- Group discussion: "Where's the line?"
- Sample syllabus statement (shared)
- **Mini-reflection:** "What would Paul or Peter or Jesus himself say about how we use AI?"

02:15–02:45 AI and Formation

- Discussion: "What kind of person am I becoming when I use AI this way?"
- Connect to telos, grit, and the "get-to" mindset
- Optional journaling prompt: "How do I want to use AI this semester—and why?"

02:45–03:00 Closing & Commissioning

- Recap key takeaways
- Invite students to commit to one practice or boundary
- Optional: Create a shared "AI Honor Code" for the group
- Closing blessing or commissioning

Sample Follow-Up Reflection: Prompt: "AI and Me—A Tool for Learning or a Shortcut from Growth?"
Instructions:
　After participating in the AI Prompting Workshop, write a 500–750 word reflection responding to the following questions. Be honest, thoughtful, and specific. This is not a technical report—it's a personal reflection on how you plan to engage with AI as a learner and future engineer.
Reflection Questions:

1. What did you learn about AI that surprised you, challenged you, or clarified your thinking?
   (Consider both technical insights and ethical implications.)

2. How have you used AI in the past—and how might your approach change after this workshop?
   (Be specific. What boundaries or practices will you adopt?)

3. What kind of learner do you want to be in the age of AI?
   (How will you balance efficiency with formation, speed with depth?)

4. How does your use of AI reflect your values, your calling, and your identity in Christ and as a t-shaped engineer?
   (Connect to technical depth, relational breadth, and Christ-centered purpose.)

5. Complete this sentence: "This semester, I will use AI to _____, but I will not use it to _____."
   (Explain your reasoning.)

INITIATIVE 4: PROPOSE A NEW GENERAL EDUCATION COURSE — "AI AND HUMAN FLOURISHING" (CHAPTER 10)

The rise of AI is not just a technical revolution—it is a philosophical and theological one. As machines increasingly perform tasks once thought to require human intelligence, we are forced to ask: What does it mean to be human? What is our work for? What is our worth when machines can outperform us in tasks we once considered uniquely ours?

This initiative proposes a new course within our University's general education core, specifically under the "Topics in Technology and Human Flourishing" category. This category is designed to foster interdisciplinary engagement with contemporary technological issues through a Christian lens. Courses in this area are expected to be team-taught, draw from multiple disciplines, and address the ethical, cultural, and theological dimensions of technology.

Goal: Create space for ethical, philosophical, and theological exploration of AI's role in society.

Rationale: Students need more than technical fluency—they need a moral center. A general education course on AI and human flourishing invites students to wrestle with the big questions: What kind of world are we building? What kind of people are we becoming? How can we use technology in ways that honor God and serve others?

This course would directly support several general education learning outcomes (note, I've listed my University's germane outcomes here—most deeply Christian institutions would have something similar in place):

- **SLO2**: Interpret the world in contemporary contexts
- **SLO4**: Deliver effective oral presentations
- **SLO6**: Demonstrate cultural competence within a theological framework
- **SLO7**: Articulate an informed Christian vision of human flourishing

It would also reinforce key ABET outcomes for engineering students:

- **ABET 3**: Communicate effectively with a range of audiences
- **ABET 4**: Recognize ethical and professional responsibilities in engineering contexts
- **ABET 5**: Function effectively on a team with leadership and collaboration

ACTION STEPS:

- Develop and submit a course proposal to the General Education Curriculum Committee.
- Suggested course title: "AI and Human Flourishing: Technology, Ethics, and the Christian Ethos."
- Core themes might include:
  - The history and future of AI: from Turing to transformers.
  - Human identity and creativity in the age of machines.
  - The anchoring framework of the t-shaped engineer
  - Theological anthropology: what Scripture says about work, wisdom, and worth.
  - AI's impact on labor, relationships, justice, and meaning.
  - Practical AI literacy: how to use AI tools wisely and ethically.

- Course assignments could include:
  - A personal technology audit and reflection.
  - A case study analysis of an AI-related ethical dilemma.
  - A final project proposing a redemptive use of AI in a chosen field.
  - A team presentation on a contemporary AI issue, integrating technical, ethical, and theological perspectives.

This initiative supports the "AI-proofing" quadrant of the 2x2 matrix by helping students develop the inner resources to resist dehumanizing uses of technology. It also reinforces the "get-to" mindset by framing learning as a journey toward wisdom, not just utility. Most importantly, it invites students to see themselves not just as users of technology, but as stewards of it—called to shape the future with clarity, courage, and Christ-centered purpose.

Additional Materials:

Sample Syllabus Excerpt:
DISC 3xx3: AI, Relational Skills, and Human Flourishing
Fall 2026 3 Credit Hours
Instructor: XXXX
Email: XXXX
Meeting Time & Location: TBD
Course Description
This interdisciplinary course explores how artificial intelligence intersects with relational skills and Christian visions of human flourishing. Students from all majors will engage technical, ethical, and theological dimensions of AI through readings, discussion, and experiential learning. Topics include vocational discernment, cultural critique, and the role of technology in shaping society. No prior technical background required.
General Education Learning Outcomes

- SLO 2: Interpret the world in historical and contemporary contexts
- SLO 4: Deliver effective oral presentations
- SLO 6: Demonstrate cultural competence within a theological framework
- SLO 7: Articulate an informed Christian vision of human flourishing in relation to technology

Course Learning Outcomes

- Explain foundational AI concepts and implications
- Demonstrate relational skills through dialogue and reflection
- Analyze cultural narratives and ethical frameworks
- Articulate a Christian vision of flourishing in the age of AI
- Develop a capstone project integrating course themes and personal vocation

Major Assignments

- Weekly Reflections & Reading Responses (20%)
- Midterm Presentation (20%)
- Capstone Project (Written + Oral) (30%)
- Participation & Discussion (20%)

Sample Textbook: *The t-Shaped Engineer in the Age of AI*

INITIATIVE 5: CULTIVATING A "GET-TO" CULTURE (CHAPTER 11)

This initiative appears last in the roadmap not because it is least important, but because it is most essential. Without a culture that frames learning as a calling rather than a chore, the other initiatives risk becoming techniques rather than transformation. Faculty development, AI literacy, ethical discernment, and curricular innovation all depend on a shared posture—a deep, communal belief that education is a gift. If this culture takes root, the rest of the dominoes are more likely to fall. But without it, even the best strategies may fail to form the kind of engineers—and people—we hope to send into the world.

In an age of automation, it is easy for students to see learning as transactional: a series of tasks to complete, hoops to jump through, or boxes to check. But Christian education calls us to something deeper. Learning is not a burden to endure—it is a gift to steward. A "get-to" mindset reframes education as a response to calling, not compulsion.

This initiative addresses the motivational crisis at the heart of the digital age. It draws on research in positive psychology, which shows that gratitude, autonomy, and meaning are key drivers of sustained engagement. It also aligns with theological anthropology: we are not machines to be optimized, but image-bearers called to love God with our minds (Mark 12:30).

Goal: Shift the mindset from obligation to vocation.

Rationale: Students who see learning as a "get-to" are more likely to persevere through difficulty, engage deeply, and connect their studies to a larger purpose. Faculty who model this mindset help cultivate a culture of joy, resilience, and worshipful curiosity.

ACTION STEPS:

- Deliver a "Welcome Back" lecture at the start of each semester that frames learning as a calling. Include testimonies from faculty and alumni. Again I note that this fits with my University culture. Your institution might deliver a different kind of anchoring, orienting, and impactful experience focused on this goal and rationale.
- Integrate "get-to" language into syllabi, advising, and classroom rituals. For example: "We get to wrestle with this problem because it matters for human flourishing."
- Encourage faculty to redesign at least one assignment per course to reflect a "get-to" framing—emphasizing creativity, relevance, or service.
- Send mid-semester encouragements to faculty with sample affirming phrases that they can use with students: "It's okay—this is supposed to be hard. That means you're learning."

Additional Materials:

Sample 'Get-To Phrases:

"We get to wrestle with this problem because it matters for human flourishing."

"You get to build something that could serve others—this isn't just a grade, it's a gift."

"We get to slow down and think deeply—because wisdom takes time."

"You get to ask hard questions here, not just answer them."

"We get to learn together—not just from the textbook, but from each other."

"You get to practice perseverance—because growth doesn't happen without struggle."

"We get to use tools like AI—but we also get to decide how they shape us."

"You get to present your ideas—not just to prove you know something, but to share something worth knowing."

"We get to connect our work to purpose, not just performance."

"You get to be formed here—not just trained."

Sample Mid-Semester Email:
Subject: Mid-Semester Nudge: "Get-To" Culture & the Gift of Friction
Dear Faculty,

As we reach the midpoint of the semester, I want to offer a gentle reminder—one rooted in our shared commitment to formation.

Students are tired. You may be too. But this is also the moment when growth is most possible. The friction they're feeling? It's not failure—it's formation. It's the sacred tension where learning takes root.

Please consider taking a few minutes in class this week to remind students:

- **They don't just have to do this—they get to.** They get to wrestle with ideas, build something meaningful, and grow in ways that matter.
- **Struggle is part of the process.** The discomfort they feel is often the signal that something important is happening.

Here are a few phrases you might use:

- "We get to do hard things here—because they shape us."
- "This isn't just a hoop to jump through. It's a chance to grow."
- "You're not just earning a grade—you're becoming someone."

Thank you for modeling presence, care, and purpose. Your posture shapes culture—and culture shapes character.

Gratefully,
Mike

APPENDIX B

MAKING IT WORK:
A CROSS REFERENCE AND TIMELINE

Initiative	Primary t-Dimension	Primary 2x2 Quadrant	Primary Audience	Implement
1. Embed AI Engagement	Technical Depth	Joyful & Wise	Faculty + Students	1 semester
2. PERMA Workshop	Relational Breadth	Purposeful & Protective	Faculty	1 day
3. AI Prompting Workshop	Technical Depth	Joyful & Wise	Students	1 session
4. Gen Ed Course	Christ-Centered Purpose	Joyful & Wise	Curric. Committee	6-12 months
5. Get-To Culture	All Three	Joyful & Wise	Everyone	Ongoing

Cross Reference and Timeline

THE END

Bibliography

ABET. *Criteria for Accrediting Engineering Programs*. Baltimore: Engineering Accreditation Commission, 1998.
ABET. *Criteria for Accrediting Engineering Programs: 2025-2026*. Baltimore: Engineering Accreditation Commission, ABET, 2025. https://www.abet.org/accreditation/accreditation-criteria/criteria-for-accrediting-engineering-programs-2025-2026/.
ABET. "Accredited Program Search." Accessed July 13, 2025. https://amspub.abet.org/aps.
Adler, Mortimer J. *The Difference of Man and the Difference It Makes*. New York: Holt, Rinehart and Winston, 1967. Reprint, New York: Fordham University Press, 1993.
Advancio Inc. "No Junior Engineers, No Problem: How AI Is Eliminating Entry-Level Dev Jobs." May 9, 2025. https://www.advancio.com/junior-engineers-are-extinct-now-what-how-to-stay-relevant-in-the-ai-powered-job-market/.
American Society of Civil Engineers. *Civil Engineering Body of Knowledge for the 21st Century: Preparing the Civil Engineer for the Future*. 2nd ed. Reston, VA: ASCE, 2008.
American Society of Mechanical Engineers. *Vision 2030: Creating the Future of Mechanical Engineering Education*. New York: ASME, 2011.
Anderson, Lorin W., and David R. Krathwohl, eds. *A Taxonomy for Learning, Teaching, and Assessing: A Revision of Bloom's Taxonomy of Educational Objectives*. New York: Longman, 2001.
Bartholomew, Craig G., and Michael W. Goheen. *The Drama of Scripture: Finding Our Place in the Biblical Story*. 3rd ed. Grand Rapids, MI: Baker Academic, 2024.
Betteridge, Biba, William Chien, Ellen Hazels, and Julianna Simone. "How Does Technology Affect the Attention Spans of Different Age Groups?" *OxJournal*, September 5, 2023. https://www.oxjournal.org/how-does-technology-affect-the-attention-spans-of-different-age-groups/.
Bjork, Robert A., and Elizabeth L. Bjork. "Making Things Hard on Yourself, but in a Good Way: Creating Desirable Difficulties to Enhance Learning." In *Psychology and the Real World: Essays Illustrating Fundamental Contributions to Society*, edited by Morton Ann Gernsbacher, 56-64. New York: Worth, 2011.
Bloom, Benjamin S., ed. *Taxonomy of Educational Objectives, Handbook I: The Cognitive Domain*. New York: David McKay, 1956.
Bransford, John D., Ann L. Brown, and Rodney R. Cocking, eds. *How People Learn: Brain, Mind, Experience, and School*. Washington, DC: National Academy Press, 2000.
Brooks, Arthur C. "How to 'Subvert the Culture' with Love." *Deseret News*, February 7, 2024. https://www.deseret.com/2024/2/7/24064812/subvert-culture-love-happiness-arthur-brooks-harvard/.

BIBLIOGRAPHY

———. "Intelligence in the Workplace: Why EQ Matters More Than IQ." *The Weir Institute*, March 7, 2025. https://weirinstitute.com/wellness/emotional-intelligence-in-the-workplace-why-eq-matters-more-than-iq/.

Brown, Tom B., Mann, Benjamin, Ryder, Nick, Subbiah, Melanie, Kaplan, Jared, Dhariwal, Prafulla, et al. "Language Models Are Few-Shot Learners." arXiv preprint arXiv:2005.14165 (2020).

Brue, Ethan J., Derek C. Schuurman, and Steven H. VanderLeest. *A Christian Field Guide to Technology for Engineers and Designers*. Downers Grove, IL: IVP Academic, 2022.

Burton, Tara Isabella. *Strange Rites: New Religions for a Godless World*. New York: PublicAffairs, 2020.

Burton, Virginia Lee. *Katy and the Big Snow*. Boston: Houghton Mifflin, 1943.

———. *The Little House*. Boston: Houghton Mifflin, 1942.

———. *Mike Mulligan and His Steam Shovel*. Boston: Houghton Mifflin, 1939.

Castelo, Noah, Kostadin Kushlev, Adrian F. Ward, Michael Esterman, and Peter B. Reiner. "Blocking Mobile Internet on Smartphones Improves Sustained Attention, Mental Health, and Subjective Well-Being." *PNAS Nexus* 4, no. 2 (2025): pgaf017. https://doi.org/10.1093/pnasnexus/pgaf017.

Centers for Disease Control and Prevention. "Youth Risk Behavior Survey." Accessed July 13, 2025. https://www.cdc.gov/healthyyouth/data/yrbs/index.htm.

Christian Engineering Society. "Member Institutions." Accessed July 13, 2025. https://www.christianengineer.org/.

Coetzer, Graeme H. "Emotional versus Cognitive Intelligence: Which Is the Better Predictor of Efficacy for Working in Teams?" *Journal of Business and Management*, 2023. https://jbam.scholasticahq.com/api/v1/articles/1161-emotional-versus-cognitive-intelligence-which-is-the-better-predictor-of-efficacy-for-working-in-teams.pdf.

Council for Christian Colleges & Universities (CCCU). "Member Institutions." Accessed July 13, 2025. https://www.cccu.org/members/.

Cox, Daniel A. "The State of American Friendship: Change, Challenges, and Loss." Survey Center on American Life, May 2021. https://www.americansurveycenter.org/research/the-state-of-american-friendship-change-challenges-and-loss/.

Crone, Eveline A., and Elly A. Konijn. "Media Use and Brain Development During Adolescence." *Nature Communications* 9 (2018): 588. https://doi.org/10.1038/s41467-018-03126-x.

de Ridder, Jeroen. "Online Illusions of Understanding." *Social Epistemology* 38, no. 6 (2024): 727–742. https://doi.org/10.1080/02691728.2022.2151331.

Devlin, Jacob, et al. "BERT: Pre-training of Deep Bidirectional Transformers for Language Understanding." *arXiv preprint* arXiv:1810.04805 (2018).

Duckworth, Angela. *Grit: The Power of Passion and Perseverance*. New York: Scribner, 2016.

Earl, Michael J. *Management Strategies for Information Technology*. Englewood Cliffs, NJ: Prentice Hall, 1989.

El-Sayed, Jacqueline, Sarah DeLeeuw, and Russell Korte. *Preparing Engineering Students for the Future: Report of the Future-Ready Engineering Ecosystem (FREE) Workshops*. Washington, DC: American Society for Engineering Education, 2024. https://free.asee.org.

Estes, Allen C., Ronald W. Welch, and Steven J. Ressler. "The ExCEEd Teaching Model." *Journal of Professional Issues in Engineering Education and Practice* 131, no. 4 (2005): 218–222.

BIBLIOGRAPHY

European Commission. *A Comprehensive Approach to Mental Health*. Brussels: European Commission, 2023. https://commission.europa.eu/topics/public-health/european-health-union/comprehensive-approach-mental-health_en.

Fink, L. Dee. *Creating Significant Learning Experiences: An Integrated Approach to Designing College Courses*. San Francisco: Jossey-Bass, 2003.

Frankl, Viktor E. *Man's Search for Meaning*. Translated by Ilse Lasch. Boston: Beacon, 2006.

Gallup, Purdue University, and the Lumina Foundation. *Great Jobs, Great Lives: The 2014 Gallup-Purdue Index Report*. Washington, DC: Gallup, 2014.

Gladwell, Malcolm. *Outliers: The Story of Success*. New York: Little, Brown and Company, 2008.

Glanzer, Perry L., and Todd C. Ream. *Christian Higher Education: An Empirical Guide*. Abilene, TX: Abilene Christian University Press, 2022.

Glanzer, Perry L., and Jesse Rine. "Operationalizing Christian Identity: A Guide for Christian Colleges and Universities." *Christian Higher Education* 20, no. 1–2 (2021): 3–23.

Glanzer, Perry L., Jesse Rine, and Todd C. Ream. *The Idea of a Christian College: A Reexamination for Today's University*. Eugene, OR: Cascade, 2022.

Glanzer, Perry L., and Nathan F. Alleman. "The OCIG Score: Measuring the Operationalization of Christian Identity in Higher Education." *Christian Scholar's Review* 52, no. 3 (2023): 201–225.

Greenfield, David N. *Virtual Addiction: Help for Netheads, Cyberfreaks, and Those Who Love Them*. Oakland, CA: New Harbinger Publications, 1999.

Guest, David. "Managers in Focus as the Skills Gap Closes, The Hunt is On for the Renaissance Man of Computing," *The Independent*, September 17, 1991.

Haliti-Sylaj, Trendeline, and Alisa Sadiku. "Impact of Short Reels on Attention Span and Academic Performance of Undergraduate Students." *Eurasian Journal of Applied Linguistics* 10, no. 3 (2024): 60–68. https://files.eric.ed.gov/fulltext/EJ1454296.pdf.

Harvard Business Publishing Corporate Learning and Degreed. *Gen AI Fluency at Work: How Organizations Unlock the Full Potential of an AI-Proficient Workforce*. Boston: Harvard Business, 2025. https://www.harvardbusiness.org/wp-content/uploads/2025/04/CRE6080_CL_Perspective_Gen-AI-Fluency_April2025.pdf.

Harvard Study of Adult Development. "What Makes a Good Life? Lessons from the Longest Study on Happiness." Harvard University, 2015. https://news.harvard.edu/gazette/story/2017/04/over-nearly-80-years-harvard-study-has-been-showing-how-to-live-a-healthy-and-happy-life/.

Hsu, Hua. "What Happens After A.I. Destroys College Writing?" *The New Yorker*, July 7, 2025. https://www.newyorker.com/magazine/2025/07/07/the-end-of-the-english-paper.

Jeong, Se-Hoon, and Yoori Hwang. "Media Multitasking Effects on Cognitive vs. Attitudinal Outcomes: A Meta-Analysis." *Human Communication Research* 42, no. 4 (2016): 599–618. https://doi.org/10.1111/hcre.12089.

Kang, Jay Caspian. "Does A.I. Really Encourage Cheating in Schools?" *The New Yorker*, August 30, 2024. https://noegret.org/wp-content/uploads/2024/10/Does-A.I.-Really-Encourage-Cheating-in-Schools_-_-nym.pdf.

Keller, Timothy. "The Decline and Renewal of the American Church." Tim Keller & Gospel in Life, 2021–2022.

———. *Every Good Endeavor: Connecting Your Work to God's Work*. New York: Dutton, 2012.

———. *The Meaning of Marriage: Facing the Complexities of Commitment with the Wisdom of God*. New York: Dutton, 2011.

———. *The Prodigal God: Recovering the Heart of the Christian Faith*. New York: Dutton, 2008.

———. *The Reason for God: Belief in an Age of Skepticism*. New York: Dutton, 2008.

Kern, Margaret L. "PERMAH: A Useful Model for Focusing on Well-Being in Schools." In *Handbook of Positive Psychology in Schools: Supporting Process and Practice*, 3rd ed., edited by Kelly-Ann Allen et al., 12–24. New York: Routledge, in press.

Kern, Margaret L., and Susan D. Benecchi. *Intersections of Positive Psychology and Christianity*. White paper, 2019. https://www.peggykern.org/uploads/5/6/6/7/56678211/kern___benecchi_2019_-_intersections_of_pospsych_and_christianity.pdf.

Kovich, Melissa K., Vicki L. Simpson, Karen J. Foli, Zachary Hass, and Rhonda G. Phillips. "Application of the PERMA Model of Well-Being in Undergraduate Students." *International Journal of Community Well-Being* 6 (2023): 1–20.

Larsen, Douglas P. "Planning Education for Long-Term Retention: The Cognitive Science and Implementation of Retrieval Practice." *Seminars in Neurology* 38, no. 4 (2018): 449–456. https://doi.org/10.1055/s-0038-1666983.

Leiffer, Paul. *Engineering Through the Lens of Faith*. Tyler, TX: LeTourneau University Press, 2023.

Lencioni, Patrick. *The 6 Types of Working Genius: A Better Way to Understand Your Gifts, Your Frustrations, and Your Team*. New York: Matt Holt Books, 2022.

———. *The Advantage: Why Organizational Health Trumps Everything Else in Business*. San Francisco: Jossey-Bass, 2012.

———. *The Five Dysfunctions of a Team: A Leadership Fable*. San Francisco: Jossey-Bass, 2002.

Leonard-Barton, Dorothy. *Wellsprings of Knowledge: Building and Sustaining the Sources of Innovation*. Boston: Harvard Business School Press, 1995.

Lewis, C. S. *Mere Christianity*. New York: HarperOne, 2001.

Lowman, Joseph. *Mastering the Techniques of Teaching*. 2nd ed. San Francisco: Jossey-Bass, 1995.

Lui, Kelvin, and Alan C. M. Wong. "Cognitive Costs of Multitasking: A Meta-Analytic Review." *Journal of Experimental Psychology: General* 149, no. 4 (2020): 665–683.

Macaulay, David. *The Way Things Work*. Boston: Houghton Mifflin, 1988.

Maczka, Darren K., and Erin J. McCave. "Integrating Computation within an Engineering Physics Course." *ASEE Annual Conference & Exposition*, 2023. https://peer.asee.org/wip-integrating-computation-within-an-engineering-physics-course.

Marinkovic, Jenai. "The Shifting Importance of Soft Skills in a Time of AI Systems, Large Language Models and Global AI Regulations." ISACA, October 9, 2023. https://www.isaca.org/resources/news-and-trends/isaca-now-blog/2023/the-shifting-importance-of-soft-skills-in-a-time-of-ai-systems.

Marzano, Robert J., Debra J. Pickering, and Daisy E. Arredondo. *Dimensions of Learning: Teacher's Manual*. 2nd ed. Alexandria, VA: Association for Supervision and Curriculum Development, 1997.

Mayer, Anne-Sophie, Reza M. Baygi, and Reinout Buwalda. "Generation AI: Job Crafting by Entry-Level Professionals in the Age of Generative AI." *Business & Information Systems Engineering* 67 (2025): 595–613. https://link.springer.com/article/10.1007/s12599-025-00959-x.

BIBLIOGRAPHY

McCloskey, Abby M. "A Christian Mind out of Practice." *Christianity Today*, June 10, 2025. https://www.christianitytoday.com/2025/06/christian-mind-out-of-practice-mark-noll-discipleship/.

McGinnis, Michael J. and Lett, Jonathan. "Engineering, Meaning and Faith: Professional Formation of Engineers with Magnitude and Direction" (2024). Christian Engineering Conference. 11.

Medhat, Sa'ad, and Sarah Peers. *T-Shaped Learning for the New Technologist*. London: NEF: The Innovation Institute, 2012. https://stemfoundation.org.uk/resource.pdf.

Microsoft. AI Diffusion Report. Microsoft AI Economy Institute, October 2025. https://www.microsoft.com/en-us/research/wp-content/uploads/2025/10/Microsoft-AI-Diffusion-Report.pdf.

Miller, Richard K. "Beyond T-Shaped: Toward A Framework for Engineering Education in the 21st Century." *Olin College White Paper*, 2015.

———. "Why the Hard Science of Engineering Is No Longer Enough to Meet the 21st Century Challenges." In *Rebalancing Engineering Education*, 77–94. Olin College of Engineering, 2015. https://undergrad.msu.edu/uploads/Rebalancing EngineeringEducationTReadingrec.pdf.

Mondal, Aritra. "Digital Distraction and Student Attention: A Qualitative Study." *Journal of Educational Technology and Society* 27, no. 1 (2024): 45–59.

National Academy of Engineering. *The Engineer of 2020: Visions of Engineering in the New Century*. Washington, DC: National Academies Press, 2004.

National Society of Professional Engineers. *Professional Engineering Body of Knowledge*. Alexandria, VA: NSPE, 2013.

Noll, Mark A. *The Scandal of the Evangelical Mind*. Grand Rapids, MI: Eerdmans, 1994.

Olson, Elsie. *AI Basics (Exploring Artificial Intelligence)*. Minneapolis: Lerner Publications, 2025.

Palmer, Colin. "'Hybrids'—A Critical Force in the Application of Information Technology in the Nineties." *Journal of Information Technology* 5, no. 4 (1990): 232–235.

Papakostas, Christos. Artificial Intelligence in Religious Education: Ethical, Pedagogical, and Theological Perspectives. *Religions* 16, no. 5 (2025): 563. https://doi.org/10.3390/rel16050563.

Paradox Learning. *AI Literacy Framework for Educators and Learning Professionals*. Calgary, AB: Paradox Learning, 2024. https://paradoxlearning.com/wp-content/uploads/2024/09/AI-Literacy-Framework_updated_071124.pdf.

Pew Research Center. *Decline of Christianity in the U.S. Has Slowed, May Have Leveled Off: Findings from the 2023-24 Religious Landscape Study*. Washington, DC: Pew Research Center, February 26, 2025. https://www.pewresearch.org/wp-content/uploads/sites/20/2025/02/PR_2025.02.26_religious-landscape-study_report.pdf.

Piper, John. *Think: The Life of the Mind and the Love of God*. Wheaton, IL: Crossway, 2010.

Plummer, James D. "Educating the Engineer of 2020." Stanford School of Engineering, 2011. (Referenced in IEEE Spectrum summary: "The Engineers of the Future Will Not Resemble the Engineers of the Past," May 30, 2017.)

Putnam, Robert D. *Bowling Alone: The Collapse and Revival of American Community*. New York: Simon & Schuster, 2000.

Rubinstein, Joshua S., David E. Meyer, and Jeffrey E. Evans. "Executive Control of Cognitive Processes in Task Switching." *Journal of Experimental Psychology: Human Perception and Performance* 27, no. 4 (2001): 763–797.

Russell, Stuart J., and Peter Norvig. *Artificial Intelligence: A Modern Approach.* 4th ed. Upper Saddle River, NJ: Pearson, 2020.

Schuurman, Derek C. "Virtue and Artificial Intelligence." *Perspectives on Science and Christian Faith* 75, no. 3 (2023): 155–161. https://www.asa3.org/ASA/PSCF/2023/PSCF12-23Schuurman.pdf.

Seligman, Martin E. P. *Flourish: A Visionary New Understanding of Happiness and Well-Being.* New York: Free Press, 2011.

Shatzer, Jacob. *Transhumanism and the Image of God: Today's Technology and the Future of Christian Discipleship.* Downers Grove, IL: IVP Academic, 2019.

Stalder, Daniel R. "What Pro-AI Educators May Overlook About Education." *Psychology Today*, June 27, 2025. https://www.psychologytoday.com/us/blog/bias-fundamentals/202506/what-pro-ai-educators-may-overlook-about-education.

Sutskever, Ilya, Oriol Vinyals, and Quoc V. Le. "Sequence to Sequence Learning with Neural Networks." *Advances in Neural Information Processing Systems* 27 (2014).

Sutton, Robert I. *The No Asshole Rule: Building a Civilized Workplace and Surviving One That Isn't.* New York: Business Plus, 2007.

Sutton, Trevor A. "AI and the Discipline of Human Flourishing." *Religion & Liberty*, Vol 34, No. 1, 2024.

Taylor, Charles. *A Secular Age.* Cambridge, MA: Belknap of Harvard University Press, 2007.

Thacker, Jason. "Why Christians Should Care about Artificial Intelligence." *WeeklyTech*, March 28, 2022. https://jasonthacker.com/2022/03/28/why-christians-should-care-about-artificial-intelligence/.

Tranquillo, Joe. "The T-Shaped Engineer." *Journal of Engineering Education Transformations* 30, no. 4 (April 2017): 1–10.

Turnitin and Vanson Bourne. *Crossroads: Navigating the Intersection of AI in Education.* Oakland, CA: Turnitin, 2025. https://www.turnitin.com/whitepapers/ai-in-education.

U.S. Department of Health and Human Services. *Our Epidemic of Loneliness and Isolation: The U.S. Surgeon General's Advisory on the Healing Effects of Social Connection and Community.* Washington, DC: Office of the Surgeon General, 2023.

U.S. News & World Report. "Best Undergraduate Engineering Programs Rankings." Accessed July 13, 2025. https://www.usnews.com/best-colleges/rankings/engineering-overall.

Vaswani, Ashish, et al. "Attention Is All You Need." *Advances in Neural Information Processing Systems* 30 (2017).

Wankat, Phillip C., and Frank S. Oreovicz. *Teaching Engineering.* New York: McGraw-Hill, 1993.

Ward, Thomas, et al. "AI Use and Academic Performance: A Multi-Institutional Study." *Educational Researcher* 53, no. 2 (2024): 112–127.

Wilcox, Laura. "Emotional Intelligence Is No Soft Skill." *Harvard Professional & Executive Development*, January 8, 2024. https://professional.dce.harvard.edu/blog/emotional-intelligence-is-no-soft-skill/.

Zhai, Chunpeng, Santoso Wibowo, and Lily D. Li. "The Effects of Over-Reliance on AI Dialogue Systems on Students' Cognitive Abilities: A Systematic Review." *Smart Learning Environments* (2024). https://doi.org/10.1186/s40561-024-00316-7.

Zimmerman, Barry J. "Becoming a Self-Regulated Learner: An Overview." *Theory into Practice* 41, no. 2 (2002): 64–70.

www.ingramcontent.com/pod-product-compliance
Lightning Source LLC
Chambersburg PA
CBHW071438150426
43191CB00008B/1163